Harper's BAZAAR FASHION

Coco: I invented "STYLE" and the world is still wearing my style...

Karl Lagerfeld 2010

❝ Coco Chanel invented style. ❞

—KARL LAGERFELD, ARTISTIC DIRECTOR, CHANEL

Harper's BAZAAR FASHION

YOUR GUIDE TO PERSONAL STYLE

LISA ARMSTRONG
EDITED BY MEENAL MISTRY

FOREWORD BY GLENDA BAILEY

HEARST BOOKS
A division of Sterling Publishing Co., Inc.

New York / London
www.sterlingpublishing.com

" Personal style comes
from within. It's
when the woman, her
individuality and
spirit, come through.
She uses clothes
to express who she is
and how she feels. "

—DONNA KARAN

"Style is personality. It's having the ability to look at things beyond fashion and the self-confidence to transform even the simplest thing into something special. It is a natural quality you cannot learn and there are no rules to follow."

—DOMENICO DOLCE
& STEFANO GABBANA

CONTENTS

FOREWORD

I LOVE THE POWER OF A RUNWAY SHOW, BUT I'M EQUALLY fascinated to see those same clothes in the office, on the street, in a restaurant. Because that's the moment where individual tastes, quirks and practical needs merge to shape Fashion into Style.

How to perfect that transformation is something I enjoy exploring every month in the pages of *Harper's Bazaar*. After all, even women who are seemingly born with razor-sharp personal style can benefit from a bit of advice, a helpful tip and of course inspiration.

And so we decided to offer our latest book, which has all of the above and then some. *Harper's Bazaar Fashion: Your Guide to Personal Style* plumbs the rich history of style setters—from Wallis Simpson to Sarah Jessica Parker—to study how they've crafted and evolved their wardrobes so as to be worthy of marvel. Reflecting back over the decades shows that personal style isn't solely a modern phenomenon. Just think of fabulous Katharine Hepburn going against the grain in the tailored trousers that suited her no-nonsense temperament.

Every chapter begins with an essay penned by Lisa Armstrong, witty and wise fashion editor of *The Times* in the U.K. and a frequent *Bazaar* contributor. They're followed by pages filled with smart, concrete ideas to guide you in how to find your ideal shopping style, organize your closet and of course know what to wear for any occasion, whether it's a board meeting or black-tie wedding. Consider it a compendium of essential information on which we encourage you to put your own spin.

I've also asked some of my favorite designers to offer the benefit of their wisdom and artistic talent. Throughout the chapters, you'll see their beautiful original sketches along with their responses to the question "What is personal style?" I'd like to thank every one of them for their generosity in contributing. I think you'll find both their words and images just as interesting and inspiring as I do.

But this book is really about you, regardless of your age, shape or budget. And I hope you'll turn to it often as a sort of trusted adviser to keep your style fabulous and always one of a kind. Enjoy.

Glenda

Glenda Bailey
Editor-in-Chief
Harper's Bazaar

CHAPTER 1

WHAT IS PERSONAL STYLE?

It's a question without an easy answer, but searching for one uncovers some very chic wisdom and ample inspiration

THE RIGHT STUFF

Great personal style is a quicksilver quality that seems to defy all rules and definition. But there are many valuable lessons to be extracted from those revered fashion icons across the ages who have all possessed a certain *je ne sais quoi*.

Y FIRST ENCOUNTER WITH A REAL-LIFE STYLE beacon was with my first job on a monthly glossy. It was Sade. The luminescent British-Nigerian singer was then one of the biggest female recording artists in the world. She turned up to a photo shoot one day with her signature look. Its parts: black hair twisted into a plait; white shirt with the collar casually flicked up; faded blue Levis; gold hoop earrings; scarlet lips; and two streaks of black liner on her lids. They all added up to an apparently simple matrix that delivered maximum impact—an impact so great it needed no help. But how? Why was it that nothing we as style professionals could add—clothes from the world's cutting-edge designers or the most artfully applied makeup—could improve the figure who had arrived that morning in her own clothes?

STYLE PROFILE
WALLIS SIMPSON

Though not a classic beauty, Wallis Simpson (pictured here in the 1930s) is a revered and often referenced fashion icon to this day. Never less than impeccably turned out, Simpson made her mark dressing in deceptively simple dresses and suits, tailored to within an inch of their lives to suit her long, slim frame. Then came the beautiful jewelry, much of it custom-made and given to her by the Duke of Windsor. No doubt Simpson's sharp wit was the final touch.

DEFINING THE UNDEFINABLE

I've mulled over that question many times in the intervening years. In the course of my career, I've had a ringside view to hundreds of lavishly and expensively dressed women. Broken into their constituent parts, the building blocks of Sade's style were the acme of democratic dressing. They weren't expensive and they certainly weren't unique. (Although that didn't mean they hadn't been chosen with immense care.) Still, the sum of those parts, underpinned by her feline grace, was infinitely great. Even to my untutored eye she looked ineffably right and timeless.

A sense of rightness. That may be as good a definition of style as any. Much like listening to a great piece of music, bearing witness to style can take you to unexpected places. It's a journey that could take you from the eccentricity of the late Isabella Blow, with her penchant for lobster hats, to the rigorous austerity of Wallis Simpson. Or from the edgy prettiness of Alexa Chung to the funky sleekness of Tory Burch. And no matter the exact spot, it leaves you satisfied with its internal logic.

If that sounds elusive, bear with me. Style *is* elusive. Sometimes it's easier defined by what it isn't. It isn't the same as being well-dressed, which is a worthy but less exalted state that can be achieved via a personal stylist. It's different from being chic, which, while a laudable and enviable trait, implies a certain severity and strictness. (It is a French invention after all.) Certain women—Katharine Hepburn and Coco Chanel come to mind—can sometimes possess both. More intriguingly still, style often has nothing to do with conventional beauty. Diana Vreeland, the legendary fashion editor of *Harper's Bazaar*, was, even by her loved ones' estimation, a *jolie-laide*. Although great style can trick you into thinking otherwise. And while many fashionable women aren't necessarily stylish, stylish women always look fashionable somehow. Those like Chloë Sevigny, Kate Moss and the

STYLE PROFILE
KATHARINE HEPBURN

Her penchant for menswear-influenced clothing went against the fashion codes of the day. But it speaks volumes that Katharine Hepburn (pictured here in 1952) turned her tailored ensembles of wide-legged trousers and natty jackets into an elegant gesture rather than a defiant one. Through her style and independent spirit, Hepburn became a sort of anti-bombshell, cutting a striking and unmistakable figure. The lesson: If it feels right, damn the prevailing trends.

> Personal style is about taking classic pieces and reinterpreting them to make them your own. A special ocelot-print coat and chic minibag, for example, can transform a tailored pair of jeans and a turtleneck into something uniquely personal.

—FRIDA GIANNINI,
CREATIVE DIRECTOR,
GUCCI

late Nan Kempner, who use fashion as their gateway to style, always keep in mind what flatters their bodies and don't follow trends slavishly.

A WIDE WORLD OF STYLE

There may not be an obvious road map to being stylish. Still, we know stylishness when we see it, even when it's beckoning to us from afar. Take for instance such decades-spanning examples as Louise Brooks's ebony bob, cupid lips and flapper dresses in the 1920s and Lauren Hutton's gorgeously gap-toothed and tousle-haired Charlie Girl of the 1970's. Both women are still relevant today. They were originators.

But if idiosyncracy is part of style's genome, that leaves the field blissfully wide open for infinite variety. There's Jane Birkin's ageless tomboy in slouchy trousers and sexy tousled hair, radiating sexiness and understated Parisian luxury. There's Daphne Guinness's bold geometry that's one part exhibitionist, two parts disciplined fashion disciple. There's Michelle Obama, whose closets of sleeveless shift dresses and belted cardigans furnish her with a look for every occasion and milieu. They might seem so disparate as to have nothing that can possibly connect them. However, there is.

More intriguingly still, style often has nothing to do with conventional beauty.

WHAT IT TAKES

What they share is a sense of fearlessness and an ability to not take themselves too seriously. They also relish the process of putting themselves together to face the world. It takes all three qualities, plus a dash of instinct, to appropriate menswear and humble jersey and turn them into a new way of dressing for the modern woman, as Chanel did in the 1920s. It takes all three to rip the feathers off the hem of your evening gown and redeploy them as a fan because you've just discovered another woman in an identical dress, as Daisy Fellowes did during the Belle Époque. Spontaneity, improvisation and a willingness to break rules are three more hallmarks of the truly stylish.

Having money to spend on clothes inevitably helps, but not having a lot of it isn't always an impediment to style. Consider the example of Gloria Guinness. When she was broke and living in Paris before the Second World War, Guinness still managed to outshine just about every other woman there in her uniform of simple black cardigans and skirts. No wonder she was known as the Ultimate.

LEARNING BY EXAMPLE

Don't commit the error of asking a style avatar what makes her stylish. Even if she can be coaxed through the portcullis of her modesty, chances are she still won't have a clue about the alchemy that resulted in her own sense of style. On the other hand, she will be able to tell you about her brilliant tailor to whom she takes all her clothes, so that even when she's

Don't commit the error of asking a style avatar what makes her stylish.

shopped from Gap or Zara, they end up fitting her perfectly and looking like a million dollars. She'll know exactly what shapes, lengths and proportions work for her. She'll have long ago figured out the colors, the vibes and the various eras of fashion reference that maximize her assets. She'll have unearthed precisely the right shade of red lipstick (Diana Vreeland), the ultimate jean shape (Kate Moss), the signature scent (Fracas if you're Isabella Blow) and the silhouette (wasp-waisted if you're Dita Von Teese) that's perfect for her.

The end results might look effortlessly serendipitous, and possibly, after years of practice, they may have become something that takes virtually no effort. But that doesn't mean the initial groundwork wasn't diligently tended to. Show me a stylish woman and I'll introduce you to someone who's scrutinized fashion magazines, looked at herself coolly in the mirror, made a mental list of her favorite labels and established a cozy relationship with one or two choice stores. And after trial and error, she has alighted on a defining trait she can make her own.

FROM THE INSIDE OUT

Inhabiting a look is another element of style. It means that however impeccable your tailored suits and dresses (Jackie Onassis and Babe Paley) or theatrical your ethnic flourishes (Millicent Rogers, the giddy 1930s socialite, philanthropist and champion of New Mexican art and clothes), your clothes never eclipse you. Rather, they become part of your aura because they're a visual expression of your personality.

It's because real style is a reflection of character that it mutates and evolves. Catherine Deneuve, for example, long ago moved on from the boxy shapes that first announced her arrival as a style maven in *Belle de Jour*. For the 1967 film, Yves Saint Laurent designed the clothes and Roger Vivier minted that delectable buckled pump. That stark minimalism wouldn't suit her softer contours now. Still, she has adhered to its tenets of simplicity, classicism and color. Her hair is shorter and its glacial blondeness more nuanced, but it remains recognizably luxuriant and glamorous. It's a textbook case of recognizing what it is about a look that works for you and translating it into a modern style vernacular. Anita Pallenberg, the original rock chick of the 1960s, and Brigitte Bardot, the woman for whom the title sex kitten was surely invented, eventually cast off their signatures too. Just as before them, Wallis Simpson and Grace Kelly learned to bend the decades' prevailing trends to their tastes and physiques. Currently, Sienna Miller is cherry-picking key directions from today's designers and weaving them into her own personal story of laid-back, runway-meets-street elegance.

A LITTLE NATURE, A LITTLE NURTURE

There are some women who are born stylish, but there are far more women who polish and perfect as they go along. The first time I went to interview a fresh-scrubbed Kate Moss, one of the most influential style makers of our time, back in 1992, I mistook her for the receptionist. What does this mean? That La Moss, then 18 and about to ink her first deal with Calvin Klein, hadn't quite grown into her look.

I'm not suggesting she wasn't naturally stylish, but with each phase of her life she's adapted, from grunge queen and a brief stint as sexy secretary (those Narciso Rodriguez pencil skirts and fitted dresses) to her habitual skinny, elegantly disheveled look. It's safe to assume she's given her image plenty of thought. Not having to think too hard about what you're wearing—another mythic hallmark of stylish women—is a luxury that comes only when you've cracked the code. Although that implies that style is a finite goal. In reality, the stylish woman's personal style is constantly evolving. Ultimately, that's what makes the journey so fascinating.

STYLE PROFILE
JACQUELINE ONASSIS

She was chic to the very end, but as first lady in a new and youthful administration, Jacqueline Onassis was a pioneer. Her colorfully soignée choices were at once wholly appropriate and incredibly inspiring as they introduced the country to French houses like Chanel and Givenchy and talented Americans like Oleg Cassini and Halston. She brought glamour and savvy to the White House with a new décor and dynamic cultural events, and her unerring sense of style and exquisite taste were an integral part in the making of Camelot.

20s

During the twenties, women threw off the tyranny of the corset, opting for a freer form of fashion expression. That meant boyish looks like straight flapper dresses and sleek, cropped hairdos à la Louise Brooks and Josephine Baker. Continuing in the spirit of rejecting old-fashioned femininity, Coco Chanel introduced such still-valid elements as menswear fabrics, jersey and sailor stripes into a woman's wardrobe.

Louise Brooks

Coco Chanel

Josephine Baker

STYLE BY THE DECADE

Greta
Garbo

Jean
Harlow

Barbara
Stanwyck

30s

After the crash of 1929, there was a return to a more classically feminine look for both day and night. In fact, the sex appeal of evening wear was ratcheted way up in shimmering gowns on actresses like Jean Harlow and Barbara Stanwyck. It was the first incarnation of what we call "Old Hollywood." Other iconic moments of the day: Greta Garbo's famous slouched fedora and Marlene Dietrich's sleek sartorial androgyny.

Marlene
Dietrich

Rita Hayworth

Ava Gardner

40s

The dueling forces of the forties were the red-lipped glamour of actresses like Rita Hayworth and Ava Gardner versus the dark spirit of the Second World War, which at one point famously required that women paint a black seam down the backs of their legs to mimic real (but unavailable) nylon stockings. The silhouette of the day focused on narrow hips and padded shoulders, while hair was elaborately curled to offset sleek, pared-down clothes. The best example? Think Lauren Bacall.

Lauren Bacall

Audrey
Hepburn

50s

With its wasp waists, ever-present gloves and full skirts (the enduring influence of Dior's New Look of 1947), fifties fashion was defined by a ladylike propriety and an immaculately groomed look. Behold the era's ideals: Audrey Hepburn's gamine elegance and Grace Kelly's aristocratic beauty.

60s

The decade came in like a begloved lamb and went out like a youthquaking lion. Its fashion revolutions spanned from the space-age mods to the feathered and fringed flower power of the hippies. As rules were being broken left and right, the era was rife with singular style, like that of rock chicks Anita Pallenberg and Marianne Faithfull and French actress Catherine Deneuve. Meanwhile, gangly model Twiggy redefined the feminine ideal.

Catherine Deneuve

Twiggy

Marianne Faithfull and Anita Pallenberg

Princess
Diana

80s

Madonna wore rubber bangles and lace downtown while Carolyne Roehm and Paloma Picasso wore Christian Lacroix poufs uptown. The eighties were an over-the-top time when, stylistically, anything seemed to go, like the not-for-the-meek designs of Thierry Mugler and Claude Montana. The counterpoint to the boldly exotic glamour of Grace Jones? The fresh-scrubbed sex appeal of Brooke Shields and the Sloane-Ranger prettiness of Princess Diana.

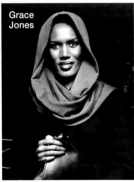

Grace
Jones

Paloma Picasso and
Carolyne Roehm

Naomi
Campbell

John F. Kennedy, Jr. and
Carolyn Bessette Kennedy

Winona
Ryder

90s

Though eighties decadence spilled over (witness Naomi Campbell here, in 1991, in the heyday of the supermodel), minimalism was the inevitable reaction to the previous decade. Enter Jil Sander, Helmut Lang and Calvin Klein—where sleek style icon Carolyn Bessette Kennedy worked before marrying John F. Kennedy Jr. Other nineties phenomena were also the result of paring down, namely the music-cum-fashion trend of grunge and the rise of the dark-clad waif à la Winona Ryder.

Sarah
Jessica
Parker

00s

Sarah Jessica Parker (as Carrie Bradshaw) brought a colorful mix of high style to the masses via *Sex and the City*, while the accessibility of both paparazzi and runway images on the Internet and the proliferation of celeb mags sealed the deal of fashion as spectator sport. The decade's influences were as vast as Mary-Kate Olsen's simultaneously luxurious and shabby layers and Michelle Obama's savvy high-low look. And of course, the emergence of fast fashion meant that everyone could participate in the game.

Michelle
Obama
and
Carla
Bruni-
Sarkozy

Mary-Kate
Olsen

29

1

WHAT IS
JE NE SAIS QUOI?

When something
is so wrong, it's right.

2

When
something
so simple is
sublime.

3

When something
classic seems new.

4

When it's effortless or just looks it.

5

I don't know,
but I like it.

STYLE PROFILE
KATE MOSS

She's the girl who launched a thousand trends. But the magic of Kate Moss is that she rarely looks trendy, even when decked out in the latest fresh-from-the-runway creations. You'll never see the supermodel-cum-designer looking overly glossed from tip to toe. There's always something slightly undone, like wearing her hair loose and natural with a beautiful vintage dress, as she is in this photograph from 2003.

HOW TO
FIND
YOUR
LOOK

Seeking a signature style
means getting to know yourself
and then getting dressed

WHERE TO START

Much like genius, personal style involves a walloping dose of perspiration to support that flash of inspiration. Creating a foundation for your look means putting in the time to learn what works best for you and your figure, as well as recognizing what you really love.

VERY DESIGNER KNOWS A SIGNATURE STYLE IS TODAY'S holy grail. In a world bursting with brands and lifestyle choices, it represents a key to selectiveness. "Elegance is refusal," as Coco Chanel said. She knew what she was talking about. Chanel spent her formative years as a designer, whittling away at the fussy carapaces of the Edwardian fashions she grew up with until she arrived at a pared-down formula that got to the essence of what it meant to be a modern woman.

THE LOOK THAT LASTS

A former muse to Yves Saint Laurent, Betty Catroux settled on her signature style decades ago. It's a slightly moody (and still inspiring) sensibility that plays the clean functionality of menswear tailoring against the tough chic of black leather in perfect harmony on her angular, long-legged frame. And of course there's her unmistakable shaggy-chic platinum-blonde hair. Catroux is proof that if you find a solid style structure, you could be set for life.

When it comes to forging a personal signature, the first step is to establish a framework. It's not a coincidence that Sarah Jessica Parker is so frequently spotted in waist-cinching full skirts, that Scarlett Johansson has developed a taste for drape-fronted bustier-style bodices and that Chloë Sevigny, for all her eclectic choices, invariably hones in on pieces that show off her stupendous legs. These women have figured out what suits their bodies as much as what sits happily with their personalities.

If style is the triumph of flair over our imperfections, then we need to know what those imperfections, as well as attributes, are. Here's where that full-length mirror starts earning its keep. Pear shape? Long neck? Short waist? Fabulous legs? Graceful arms and collarbones? Plump knees but glorious ankles? Be honest with yourself.

TAKING STOCK, MAKING NOTE

Gazing at your own reflection with a checklist may seem indulgent, but it could be one of the most productive exercises you ever undertake, saving both time and money in the long run. If you're unsure whether your waist is long or short, then ask someone who knows about these things. Today's personal shoppers are generally founts of useful knowledge and tips. Better still, they're usually free of charge.

Don't discount all those compliments you've had over the years either. Rather than blushing and brushing them off, focus on what they were telling you. Beautiful back? Lovely hands? Gorgeous mouth? There are accessories and clothes that can help you accentuate all of these. Sometimes a new haircut, as well as being transformative, can prove to be the key to unlocking a new identity. Before her elfin crop, Carey Mulligan was just another pretty starlet. Post crop, she tapped into a head-turning talent for

Pinpointing your BODY SHAPE will ELIMINATE many a wild goose chase and deliver you onto the path to CLOSET CONTENTMENT

LONG LIVE

INDIVIDUALITY

♡

ALBER

wearing quirky but instant classics. Moral: Pinpointing your body shape will eliminate many a wild goose chase and deliver you onto the path to closet contentment.

RULES OF PROPORTION

Talking about proportion in terms of style may not be the sexiest subject, but it's difficult to stress how much of a difference getting it right can make. Take heart. Few people are shaped exactly right. There are many individual quirks that women encounter. One might have a swimmer's shoulders, while another might have arms that are a touch too long. But then there are also a few rules of thumb for common body types.

Pear-shaped women should avoid pencil skirts, capri pants, drainpipes and jackets and tops that cut them at the thigh, which is their widest point. Though it's counterintuitive, they should avoid wearing all one color, as this draws the eye to the outline. Mixing light and dark colors, with light on top to flatter the complexion and darker below the waist to minimize bulges, is much more clever. The same goes for juxtaposing prints and patterns. Optically, the goal is to avoid creating a very narrow point at either the knees or the ankles, as this emphasizes hips and thighs.

Boyishly shaped women with no waists should also avoid pencil skirts, as well as wrap dresses, which are best left to women with a bosom. Similarly, voluminous clothes can make them look emaciated. What they can wear: all those directional fashion trends, tube dresses, mini hems and stripes. Slim trousers with a high heel and a curvy jacket create the illusion of a waist, while a blousy peasant top over drainpipes worn with a smart jacket will show off long legs and disguise any boniness up top.

Full-figured women should avoid both the skintight and the baggy.

They should also steer clear of overworked pieces, including bows, frilly collars and exaggerated shoulder pads, which will make a gal look bigger. Boots that cut the calves in half, or any tight boot, are an unnecessary cruelty, as are spindly straps on sandals. If your arms are less toned than you'd like, sleeveless tops go out the window. What will flatter: well-cut tunics in beautiful fabrics, pleated trousers with a straight or slightly flared leg, gently tapered jackets, drapey coats and soft dresses with subtle tailored structure as opposed to rigid corseting.

BUILDING ON A FASHION FOUNDATION

If this sounds too earthbound an approach to something as subtle as style, that's because it's only part of the story: the foundation. Once you've established the basis of a uniform, whether it's a closet that majors in tailored jackets and jeans or shirtwaisted dresses and jeweled cardigans, you can begin breaking rules. You can even go so far as to create an impression of controlled anarchy with wild accessories, provided you are ruthlessly clearheaded about flattering proportions and colors.

It should be noted, however, that style is much more than the sum of physical constraints. It's a psychological expression of temperament, which requires us to develop an instinct rather than apply inflexible laws. In theory, Kate Moss should steer clear of strappy dresses that highlight her flat chest, Kelly Osbourne shouldn't wear skirts above the knee, and Vivienne Westwood should forsake gold overalls and marmalade-colored hair. But in every case, they're so confident in their so-called shortcomings that they carry off their supposed transgressions with triumphant poise. That, in turn, becomes part of their unique look. It's surely one of the defining qualities of style.

1

STEPS TO SIGNATURE STYLE

Do the math.
Know your proportions.

2

Seek a uniform
that flatters.

3

Jettison everything
that doesn't.

4

Determine your likes and dislikes.

5

If it feels right,
go ahead and break
the rules.

ALL ABOUT YOU

Admittedly these are exceptionally assured women. But with a little lateral thinking (and a good alterations service), it's possible to transpose the spirit of any aesthetic into a reality that works for you. For instance, if you're set on the idea of a femme fatale but have a body that more obviously lends itself to the tomboy school of dressing, then you can learn from Jennifer Aniston. The actress dresses for a (deluxe) gym by day but at night turns seductive with slinky, minimalist designs that tap into her preference for the understated. Even when she's wearing head-to-toe sequins, the shape of her dress is simple, her hair and makeup uncontrived.

Ask yourself: What is it about that fashion-magazine spread or trend that you love? Is it the item or the mood it evokes?

But even before that, make a pointed effort to learn to recognize what it is you really like. That may sound like a given, but so often trends can cloud judgment. Not every trend will be for you. Sometimes you have to make peace with a hot new idea and move on. Other times, you'll be able to extrapolate the salient features—a bag, a shoe, a smattering of sequins, a swish of fringe—and incorporate them into your personal style mandate. Ask yourself: What is it about that fashion-magazine spread or trend that you love? Is it the item or the mood it evokes? The fabric or the cut? Or both? Identify the core appeal, then you can start to adapt. Ultimately, it comes down to knowing yourself both inside and out. Where there's a will, there's a way to style.

66 For me, personal style
is about that crazy
composition. It's what
I love about fashion.
A bit boyish, but a bit
sensual. A bit street,
but a bit couture.
It's all about deliberate
nonchalance. 99

—VERA WANG

CLASSIC CHIC

Embracing timeless elegance without the frippery, this look is all about being adept in injecting a subtle fresh twist to a wardrobe of exquisite sartorial standards.

• HAUTE STUFF
If you're not shopping for trendy fare, you have an opportunity to invest in quality pieces. Plus, it's counter-intuitive, but simple clothes aren't as easy to get right as those with bells and whistles.

• THE YOUTH MOVEMENT
Don't age yourself before your time. Add flair with a touch of animal print or a utilitarian accessory. Both look of-the-moment but still stand the test of seasons.

• FACE FACTS
Heavy makeup and overdone hair can turn a clean and classic look into a stuffy affair. Go lightly with the pancake and lipstick, and make sure your hair doesn't approximate a helmet in any way.

Sienna Miller

Claudia Schiffer

Carla Bruni-Sarkozy

Queen Rania of Jordan

Helena Christensen

Kirsten Dunst

ROMANTIC NOTIONS

This slightly dreamy dresser is always up for a swirl of embroidery or embellishment, especially if it recalls faraway places. But doing it right means not getting *too* wrapped up in the fairy tale.

- **CLOTHES, NOT COSTUMES**
  Bohemian looks can easily go overboard. Make sure your ensemble doesn't channel a Renaissance fair.

- **ORDINARY EXTRAS**
  Create a counterpoint with sleek and simple accessories.

- **SWEET LUXURY**
  A hippie inspiration sometimes reads down-at-the-heels. Adding the occasional but style-appropriate touch of glamour, like a beautiful pair of high-heeled boots or a shaggy fur vest, will elevate a laid-back look to elegance.

Georgina Chapman

Christy Turlington

MINIMALIST MODE

Less is infinitely more in this woman's modern and streamlined world. But excising all excess means that what's left has to work precisely and rigorously. The payoff? Sublime simplicity.

- **SHE'S COME UNDONE**
  Resist the urge to fill empty space. The absence of extraneous pieces will speak volumes.

- **BEAUTY CALLS**
  An austere aesthetic extends to hair and makeup. Keep it neat and clean with just a hint of gloss or color.

- **COLOR SCHEMES**
  When trinkets are trimmed away, you can use a range of hues—from icy pales to rich jewel tones—to add interest and keep things fresh. Also play with unexpected color combinations as part of this stylish simple plan.

Angelina Jolie

Chloë Sevigny

Tilda Swinton

Kate Bosworth

Amanda
Harlech

Cate
Blanchett

Skala
Monroque

Isabel
Toledo

MAVERICK ELEGANCE

This fearless fashion lover seems to dress by instinct and never imitation. She's not afraid to be looked at, to ignore the rules and to follow her own sartorial code.

• REALITY CHECK

Translating runway dramatics into real life isn't always a smooth road. Make statement pieces your own by adding a personal twist.

• YOURS FOREVER...

Or at least more than a couple seasons. Buy strong pieces that you truly love. You'll be able to put them away and happily sport them years later.

• STAR WARS

You're accustomed to frequently and happily being the center of attention, but take a light touch when it's someone else's turn to shine. That means you shouldn't arrive at a wedding having outdone the bride.

47

GWYNETH PALTROW

The actress has always been a fashion girl
(and designer favorite), even as she's tried on various looks,
from retro fifties elegance to of-the-minute chic.

1996

1999

2002

2004

2008

2010

1996 She may have been an ingénue but Paltrow proved a red carpet force to be reckoned with in a velvet Gucci suit.

1999 Paltrow channeled another elegant blonde actress, Grace Kelly, in a pink Ralph Lauren gown for her Oscar win.

2002 Her moody moment courtesy of an Alexander McQueen gown didn't win raves but proved she wasn't afraid to try something unexpected.

2004 Paltrow opted for a softer sophistication in a ribbon-tied Lanvin dress.

2008 Paltrow wowed both the masses and fashion savants in leg-baring looks right off the runway like this lace dress.

2010 Another day, another premiere. The actress maintained her sexy and confident style, but in a sleek and minimal body-hugging sheath with a slightly more modest hemline.

VICTORIA BECKHAM

Even as she's gone from Posh to posh, the Spice Girl-turned-designer hasn't flagged in her devotion to a fully conceived ensemble.

2000

2003

2004

2000 Though the Spice Girls had disbanded, Beckham played the global pop star to a T in a hot-pink jumpsuit.

2003 Beckham livened up a gangster-worthy pinstriped suit with bright, sunny doses of coordinated color.

2004 Though her *nom de pop* suggests she's always had a thing for luxury, she upped the ante here, carrying an Hermès Birkin bag with distressed denim.

2006 A mod moment as Beckham's style turned more sophisticated and precise.

2007 Beckham's penchant for matching accessories became infallibly chic with this Azzedine Alaïa dress and neutral pumps.

2009 With her own line of dresses a critical success, Beckham can indulge her sense of drama with bona fide high-fashion credibility—and in a gown of her own design.

CHLOË SEVIGNY

The charm of Sevigny's singular and ever-refined style is that she's able to flip an aesthetic U-turn without ever appearing out of character.

1998

2000

2001

2004

2007

2009

1998 The actress (and sometime designer) loves to put her own spin on venerable classics like the trench.

2000 One of Sevigny's powers is to not let a recognizable look, like this dress by Alber Elbaz for Yves Saint Laurent, trump her personality.

2001 Her choice of Chanel haute couture for the Oscars was bold but infallibly chic.

2004 Sevigny wears a colorful va-va-voom dress with undone hair and a sense of ease.

2007 The actress is typically fearless about wearing strong doses of color, including chartreuse.

2009 Even before it was de rigueur, Sevigny wore shorts for both day and evening with impeccable flair and of course her enviably perfect legs.

RIHANNA

After the pop sensation was discovered in 2004, her star has risen rapidly, as has her talent for wearing edgy and avant-garde fashion with a capital F.

2005

2006

2007

2008

2009

2010

2005 The fresh-faced singer wore typical teenage streetwear to an industry party.

2006 What a difference a year makes. Rihanna shifts from dirty denim to a sweetly elegant dress and patent pumps.

2007 With a sleek new haircut and a developing taste for fashion, the singer was chic in a Gucci runway look.

2008 Rihanna turns punk pretty in a bustier and jeans.

2009 Rihanna took the Paris shows by storm, sporting looks by each designer whose show she attended, like this tux jacket and harem pants at Balmain.

2010 This sculptural dress from Viktor & Rolf cements a reputation for look-at-me looks.

DAPHNE GUINNESS

- **SHORT STUFF**
  Guinness's style might seem
  out of the ordinary, but in fact
  there's a clear framework.
  One common element: hems
  a few inches north of the knee
  on body-skimming skirts and
  dresses.

- **PERFECT PLATFORMS**
  It took some time, but the
  diminutive Brit finally found the
  perfect design of Mary Jane
  platform pumps, which she
  frequently wears in various
  colors.

- **COVER GIRL**
  Guinness often layers her slim
  shifts with crewneck cardigans
  or refined little jackets.

- **MULTITASKING JEWELS**
  Guinness dips into her collection of antique brooches
  as a styling element to finish
  a look. A couple of sparkling
  beauties could end up
  fastening a scarf or glitzing up
  her neckline or even her hair.

INES DE LA FRESSANGE

- **LEAN, MEAN MENSWEAR**
  The French model-turned-fashion-executive has an attenuated physique that's ultrachic in tailored jackets and slim trousers and jeans, which have become her uniform.

- **BALLET FLATS**
  As president of Roger Vivier, she's not spoiled for choice when it comes to footwear. But at five foot eleven, de la Fressange opts for all manner of delicate but down-to-earth shoes.

- **SOMETHING OFF-KILTER**
  The former muse to Karl Lagerfeld couldn't possibly be a one-note dresser. She keeps her classics cool by adding pieces like an over-the-top sequined jacket or even whimsical bobbles atop her shoes.

PROPORTION RULES
DRESSING A CURVY BODY

- **KEEP YOUR CONTOURS**
  Show off curves with fitted—though not too tight—clothes. (A voluminous silhouette works only on angular figures.)

- **GO SOFT OR STRUCTURED**
  If the cut of a dress is slightly fluid, opt for materials that move, like cotton jersey, silk charmeuse or light-weight wools. However, something like a body-skimming shift dress should be cut in a stronger fabric to give support and create a smooth silhouette.

Halle Berry

Scarlett Johansson

- **REMEMBER YOUR LINES**
  That's as in neckline and hemline. A low scooped or plunging neck always flatters. Although be careful not to display too much of your natural assets. Showing a little leg in skirts or dresses that end just above the knee is a smart strategy. But remember, with exposure, balance is key.

- **THE MIDDLE PATH**
  If you boast an hourglass shape, highlight your waist. Dresses with a gently nipped-in waist or cinched with a belt look terrific always. Don't make the belt too tight. You should be able to sit down and breathe!

Christina Hendricks

Jennifer Hudson

Sofia Coppola

Michelle Williams

Audrey Tautou

Freida Pinto

DEFINING A BOYISH SHAPE

- **BODY BY DESIGN**

  Leave it to your clothes to create your shape. Bustier details, gathered waists, flaring peplums, sculptural ruching or pleating and well-placed ruffles can all work to give the impression of a more feminine figure.

- **BLOUSY, NOT BAGGY**

  Volume is an excellent tool to disguise a lack of curves, but there's often a fine line between stylish and sacklike. Keep a balance with formfitting details and avoid anything too oversized.

- **TOP IT OFF**

  Jackets are the best weapon in your sartorial arsenal, particularly in sturdy, structured fabrics like tweed. A sharp-cut blazer or boxy topper creates a beautiful silhouette with both slim trousers and wide-legged pants.

- **FORM A PATTERN**

  From stripes to florals to plaids, prints breathe life into a look. Don't be afraid to mix them up and have some fun.

MAXIMIZING A TALL FRAME

• MINIS AT A MINIMUM

Many trends read extremely well on statuesque physiques, like midi lengths and long, languid layers. Miniskirts and dresses, however, require delicate handling. Wear them with flats, possibly tights, and a covered-up top or just limit your hemlines to a couple inches north of the knee.

• FEMININE, NOT FROU FROU

Even if girlish frills are the look of the moment, steer clear of anything that seems pubescent. It will read awkwardly on a tall frame.

• DON'T BAN HEELS

While conventional wisdom might dictate that you don't need any more height, the proportion of high-heeled shoes is actually best on tall figures. But perhaps leave the six-inch platforms to shorter gals.

• KEEP FROCKS SOLID

Feel free to spin the color wheel from dark to bright, but monotone dresses or ones with tiny, subtle micropatterns are a far chicer option than bold graphic and splashy prints. Wear the latter in small doses.

Nicole Kidman

Rachel Roy

Brooke Shields

L'Wren Scott

Ashley Olsen

Reese Witherspoon

Christina Ricci

Tory Burch

GETTING PETITE PERFECT

• GO TO EXTREMES

Midi lengths look dowdy on diminutive figures. Your best hemline starts at the knee and then rises from there. Or head straight in the other direction with a floor-skimming maxi.

• NIP AND TUCK

Drowning in a too-big dress or pants that need hemming can make you seem like a little girl playing dress-up. Even small tailoring tweaks, like taking sleeves up an inch or two, can make a major impact.

• DON'T OVERLOAD LAYERS

Piling on hefty furs and languid knits might be de rigueur, but they easily overwhelm small frames. Keep in mind the old fashion adage: Take one thing off before you leave the house.

• TREAD CAREFULLY WITH HEELS

Wearing high heels is a petite girl's most obvious fix. But the massive scale of skyscraping platforms can look awkward with not-so-long legs. A rule of thumb: If the length of a heel is more than half your calf, look for a lower version.

CHAPTER 3

THE ART OF SHOPPING

Buying clothes intelligently
requires both a solid strategy
and a touch of savoir faire

BUILDING
A WARDROBE

There is a step in between cracking your personal fashion code and looking your stylish best: finding the clothes with which to do so. Mastering the skill that it takes to navigate the retail waters and then maintain an efficient closet is crucial.

ULIA ROBERTS'S EVENTUAL VICTORY OVER THE HAUGHTY Rodeo Drive sales staff in *Pretty Woman* has become one of the great put-downs in celluloid history. The highly memorable scene underlines a universal truth: Shopping is not always fun. However, it is an important element to achieving great style. And understanding how to do it well can keep it from being a task that isn't overly time-consuming or painful.

THE WONDERS OF WINDOW SHOPPING

In *Breakfast at Tiffany's*, Audrey Hepburn visited her favorite jewelry emporium mostly for a pick-me-up. But mounting a retail reconnaissance mission can do more than just lighten your mood. Consider it research. Hit the stores early in the season to check out the wares and get a full picture of what's available. You can always plunk the plastic down later.

"Personal style
is being yourself."

—DIANE
VON FURSTENBERG

YOUR MASTER OF THE SHOPPING UNIVERSE

Since the days of America's sweetheart playing a hooker with a heart of gold, sales associates have evolved. It's worth seeking out one with whom you click. The gifted ones are a sort of trusted fashion therapist. They understand what you're looking for even if you can't articulate it. They can suggest ways of updating your style. They can track down specific items. They can put together a versatile outfit or an entire closet.

At their absolute finest, they will gauge whether you're the type who appreciates weekly updates about what has come into the store or whether you prefer a less obtrusive approach. And they will do all this without making you feel pressured into buying everything that's set out before you.

The gifted ones are a sort of trusted fashion therapist. They understand what you're looking for even if you can't articulate it.

The key to success is to tap into whatever expertise is available. Personal shoppers or in-house stylists offer one of the best deals in the service industry and you can find them at all levels, including fast-fashion stores. They are mostly free of charge and will fetch, carry, inspire, commiserate and explore the farthest reaches of the stock room to find those special items that might not ever make it to the shop floor. A good one will happily put something aside for a couple of days while you think about it.

It's also important to approach your shopping methodically which is the ideal way to navigate the plethora of choices that bombard the average fashion customer. Choices are good, but only if you have the time and energy to discriminate between them.

CLICKS OR BRICKS?
AND OTHER IMPORTANT QUESTIONS

How and where you shop are pivotal to your enjoyment of shopping. Some women live for a small boutique where an engaged owner oversees every step. She can be a useful ally who will reward your loyalty by buying labels that specifically work for you. The relationship between Ikram Goldman, owner of Ikram in Chicago, and her most famous customer, Michelle Obama, shows how fruitful these arrangements can be.

The relationship between Ikram Goldman, owner of Ikram in Chicago, and her most famous customer, Michelle Obama, shows how fruitful these arrangements can be.

A department store may seem less intimate, but it probably carries more lines and offers a wider range of prices, which makes it easier to buy everything in one trip. Shopping online is even more impersonal, but for some women that is precisely the appeal. It can also help you live out fantasies while doing your homework. One woman I know worships her bookmarked site because it allows her to spend a putative fortune. She places her heart's desires in the basket and lets them sit there a few days. Then she puts them all back after finding cheaper versions at H&M or Zara. Another friend does all her shopping online. She orders everything in two or three sizes. Being able to try things on in the relaxed atmosphere of her home more than compensates for the inconvenience of having to return the unwanted items.

In other words, know thy foibles and find the right retail fit. Are you

WHERE TO SHOP

DEPARTMENT STORES • With a wide-ranging selection and generous return policies, department stores are the perfect place to start shopping for the season. You can get a good overview of all the new seasonal styles that are available and pick up staples like lingerie, denim and T-shirts all in one trip.

BOUTIQUES • Small shops have a tighter range of wares, but if you find one that fits you to a T, going elsewhere could be superfluous. There's also a focus on personal service, which is an advantage if you crave assistance. If not, the attention could be off-putting. One caveat: Boutiques often don't allow full returns, only exchanges or store credit.

ONLINE • You can't try on before buying, nonetheless shopping online has many charms. It's efficient. You're not limited by region. And most sites have a handy wish list feature that allows you to set aside pieces to buy later. The hassle of returns by mail is offset by very helpful customer service.

VINTAGE & RESALE • Even if you don't consider your style retro, a well-merchandised vintage shop still offers a viable option to find that one-of-a-kind look. Resale stores carry used pieces from just a few seasons ago. If you don't mind wearing trends ever so slightly past their prime, a good one could be a gold mine.

someone who needs the courage that comes from shopping in a small pack of trusted friends? Or are you a lone wolf, texting the odd picture to your particular style guru when you have the occasional flash of indecision? Are you carried away by the moment, setting out to buy a jacket but returning with a pair of thigh-high boots because you loved the way they were styled in the store? (If that is the case, the more rational and sanitized environment of online shopping could benefit you.) Or do you march forth with brave intentions but return with yet another pair of black pants? (A sensitive and hip personal shopper could be your solution.) Do you have

Part of shopping smart is timing. Retail runs on a particular, if not always entirely logical, calendar.

expensive tastes and an eye for quality but limited funds? If so, vintage could be your answer. With online sites such as atelier-mayer.com and the pricey but exquisite One Vintage on net-a-porter.com, it's becoming easier and less time-consuming to source unique pieces without having to trawl dusty, overcrowded racks.

BEYOND THE RUNWAY

Part of shopping smart is timing. Retail runs on a particular, if not always entirely logical, calendar. Spring collections arrive in stores as early as late January, while fall clothes begin trickling in as summer is dying out. It's not a bad idea to check these out while they're still fresh, whether you're serious about buying something or not. Consider it a recon mission. You can let the ideas of the season percolate before actually buying weeks later. Of course, the major collections provide the headline-grabbing soufflés, but for meat and potatoes, don't forget the precollections sandwiched in between them. There's resort, which hits racks in late November, and prefall, which starts in May. Confused? Don't worry about the details. Just know that designers offer more than what you see in magazines. Many labels now offer limited or exclusive lines that distill the brand's core values into tightly edited capsule collections of classic pieces, usually at lower prices, such as Yves Saint Laurent's Editions 24. Other designers do one-offs or slight variations for different stores.

WHEN TO CHARGE AND WHEN TO RETREAT

It's also a savvy strategy to take the time to discover which designers and brands cut the best trousers or jackets for you and to cultivate an awareness of your personal staples. The latter are worth buying in multiple, especially if you stumble across a good deal. These bulk-buy items may include perfect fitting white T-shirts, well-cut lingerie, quality hosiery, beautiful sleepwear, cashmere and gloves. Although, however much you love an item, you probably need fewer than you think.

Once you accept the notion that less really is more, you will be liberated from the burden of having to snap up every bargain. You'll be able to walk away. Truly, this is one of the best routes of all toward retail contentment. Most stylish women will tell you it's rarely the items they didn't buy that they regret. If you experience a scintilla of indecision, go away and think about it. If you're still thinking (or even lusting) twenty-four hours later, it's earned its place in your life.

FALL

- 1 trench coat
- 1 wool or tweed blazer
- 3 neutral cardigans
- 1 light cashmere scarf
- 1 silk day dress
- 1 pair of wool trousers

WARD

ESSEN

SPRING

- 1 lightweight leather jacket
- 3 blouses (silk or cotton)
- 2 skirts
- tees and tanks to layer
- 1 raincoat
- 1 pair of dark denim jeans

WINTER

- 1 tailored wool coat
- 1 shearling vest
- 1 heavy-duty parka
- 2 cashmere turtlenecks
- 1 long chunky cardigan-cum-coat
- 1 wool dress

ROBE
TIALS

SUMMER

- 3 cotton dresses
- 2 lightweight cardigans
- 1 cotton blazer
- 2 pairs of cotton trousers
- tees and tanks
- 2 silk blouses

BUY and HOLD

beautifully made pieces for the long-term.

THE BLUE-CHIP STRATEGY

WHY INVEST? • The blue-chip item is exactly what it sounds like: a strategic purchase that's worth its lofty price tag, lasts a long time and preserves—and in some cases increases—its value. Why buy one? If you do the math on the cost per wear, that Verdura cuff or Cartier Tank Francaise might not be as expensive as you think.

THE TIMELESS ZONE • A show-stopping designer piece could potentially be a blue-chip buy if you've fallen irrevocably in love with it. But that's a rare case. What you're looking for are evergreen classics from venerable brands that will work today *and* fifteen years from now.

STATUS OR SUBSTANCE? • Yes, dangling an Hermès Birkin from your arm may telegraph a certain message about wealth and the strata you might occupy in society. However, you're not merely buying bragging rights, but also a ne plus ultra piece of craftsmanship that's increasingly rare these days. It's the quality that matters, and that assures longevity.

ENTERING THE MARKET • What to buy first? Well, as judicious a move as investment shopping is, when deciding what to buy you should follow your heart. If you're going to save up your money for a single piece that could instead be spent on five items, then that piece should take your breath away just to behold it.

THE SIGNATURE PIECE

• A STYLE OF ONE'S OWN

Every so often, you come across a unique item—perhaps in a vintage store, perhaps elsewhere—that speaks to you and you simply have to have it. Then the more you wear it, the more you want to wear it. It garners compliments and green-eyed glances from friends. It quickly becomes a crucial part of your wardrobe, miraculously working with a canyon-wide range of existing clothes over the course of years. It is your signature piece.

• TO SEEK OR NOT?

Setting out to purposefully find a piece of clothing or an accessory that fits all the above criteria will likely be unfruitful. But know that such things do exist. The mysterious ways of the fashion universe helped model-slash-singer Agyness Deyn find the button-bedecked leather motorcycle jacket that she wears everywhere from black-tie events to onstage when she's rocking out. The same goes for the exquisitely beat-up brown cowboy boots that French actress, singer and fashion icon Charlotte Gainsbourg has sported for years to no less than Parisian fashion shows and photo ops at Cannes.

Agyness Deyn, at a screening in 2009

...and the CFDA Awards, 2009

Charlotte Gainsbourg at the Cannes Film Festival in 2009

...at a fashion show in 2008

...and at another fashion show in 2010

Out-of-the-ordinary details like a witty trompe l'oeil motif or exotic embellishment could signal a future signature piece.

79

BARGAIN HUNTING

BALANCE YOUR BUDGET • Everything in your wardrobe can't be a break-the-bank investment piece. It is necessary to stretch your dollar. The good news is that now more than ever, there's an an abundance of well-priced and well-made merchandise to be found from both up-and-coming labels and fast-fashion megastores, where you can snag simple staples and try out the latest trend without a hefty cash commitment.

NAVIGATING SALES • Sales are not created equal. There are far too many instances where shoppers are seduced by slashed price tags, only to get an item home and relegate it to the back of the closet. The question to ask yourself is whether you would have bought the item at its full price. If the answer is yes, then go ahead. If it's no, shelve the piece in question.

THE INTRIGUING WEB • The above advice also holds true for a relatively new shopping paradise, the Internet sample sale. A growing number of sites like Gilt Groupe and HauteLook host limited-time-only sales of designer surpluses. There are fantastic deals to be had, but don't let the pressure of a ticking clock sway your clear-eyed shopping mentality. There's always another sale right behind.

1 THE CLOSET COMMANDMENTS

Organization is the best-kept secret to great style.

2 Like with like. Group tops, skirts and so on.

3 When spring is sprung, stow the sweaters. Rewind for winter.

4 If the shoe (or other item) fits, it stays. If not, it goes.

5 Always keep it streamlined. Wardrobe excess isn't chic.

CHAPTER 4

A WARDROBE THAT WORKS

The modern office gives
the weekday wardrobe plenty of
room for fresh ideas

A FINE BALANCE

What to wear to work is an issue that's more complicated than merely adhering to a dress code. The good news: It's an opportunity to express your individual style. The not-so-good: It's easy to misstep. But there are guidelines to getting it right every time, no matter what the workday might hold.

W E SPEND A SOBERING AMOUNT OF TIME AT work. Many of us spend an even more sobering amount of time in a modern state of limbo, between official work and true leisure time. We may take a call from a different time zone, fire off half a dozen e-mails and listen to four urgent messages on our cell phones all before we've even left the house. No wonder there are as many dress-code nuances as there are workplaces.

A DRESS CODE OF ONE'S OWN

Diane von Furstenberg started her own fashion company at the tender age of 24, quickly turning her signature jersey wrap dress into a global phenomenon and a business power-house. But no matter that she was featured on the front page of *The Wall Street Journal*, you couldn't expect the designer who coined the motto "Feel like a woman, wear a dress" to don a mannish skirt suit with shoulder pads. Photographed here at work in her New York showroom in 1976, von Furstenberg is resolutely feminine. What to wear to the office is always a fluid proposition.

THE NEW(ISH) RULES

These are curious times. You can run a multibillion-dollar software company dressed in wrinkled chinos and a baseball cap, leaving the suits to the accountants and support staff. However, to say that the old mores about power dressing à la Melanie Griffith in *Working Girl*, lumbering beneath outsize shoulder pads and a bad perm, have been subverted is an oversimplification. In some offices, a beautifully cut suit still scores top points. Condoleezza Rice's pin-sharp ensembles remain a point of reference. For other industries, such as advertising, fashion and the creative sections of the media, an awareness of current trends matters.

Still, even if you have the luxury of being able to wear whatever you like to work, some women find it helpful to compartmentalize. In theory they can wear sweatshirts, but it may not engender the necessary rigor. Some unemotional auditing can be helpful, balancing what you feel is expected against what makes you comfortable.

ESTABLISHING WHAT WORKS AT WORK

Rationalize, strategize, streamline. Does it look good? Does it make you feel good? And exactly what is appropriate nowadays? A starting point is anything that isn't sexually provocative. You'd think that goes without saying, but many young women get this wrong. Still, this is not about burying your sexuality. A polished pair of heeled pumps, with bare legs in summer or dark-gray hose in winter, keep your femininity in the picture. And as proved by Michelle Obama, bare toned arms have become not only a chic way to break up a dark outfit with some skin but also a new symbol of power that's at least as potent as shoulder pads once were.

As a rule of thumb, the best cues come from your boss. If she's immacu-

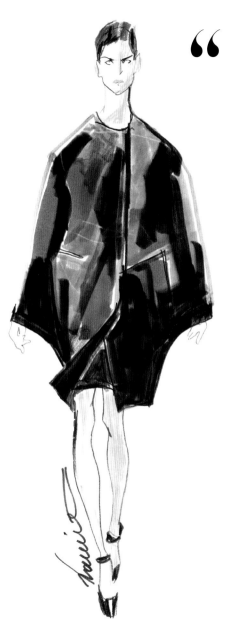

“ Personal style is about projecting ease and confidence and knowing it's all in the proportions. **”**

— FRANCISCO COSTA, WOMEN'S CREATIVE DIRECTOR, CALVIN KLEIN COLLECTION

late, then make time for grooming. If she has a slightly haphazard attitude about her appearance, then a low-key approach, without compromising your own standards, is wise. Don't sublimate your personality, but develop a complementary style. It is basic modern-business etiquette. Focus on signals over specifics. Do your colleagues' flannel pants and fine-gauge crewnecks ooze relaxed authority? Then think about how you could mirror that in your own way. Perhaps it's with a straight, dark skirt, a

Personal style is having the confidence to be who you are, not necessarily flamboyant or eccentric. It can be as simple as turning up a cuff or the contradiction of a weathered motorcycle jacket slung over an elegant evening dress. It's taking a risk, trying something unexpected, and having fun with fashion, but always being true to yourself.

—RALPH LAUREN

pretty blouse and a pair of wedge shoes (an idiosyncratic alternative to heeled pumps). Perhaps the office vibe is more iconoclastic. In that case you'd be amazed how useful a well-cut leather jacket can be. If conservative glamour is the look, then a dress, whether sheath, tunic, pinafore or wrap, with a considered cover-up is hard to beat. Identifying a uniform, however loosely you end up interpreting it, is a useful exercise because it helps you to concentrate on investment pieces.

THE FINER POINTS, PART 1

Matching suits have become more useful as an elegant cocktail option than as work wear, but good tailoring is always a sound purchase. One fabulously timeless jacket is where the bulk of your investment should go. There are many labels worth exploring, from high-end designers like Givenchy and Céline to affordable labels like Zara and J. Crew. Find something in a medium or lightweight wool, since you don't want a jacket that spends most of its office life draped over the back of your chair.

This will provide the tabula rasa for half a dozen looks, from the smart (paired with a skirt or trousers) to the quirky (over a vintage dress) to the directional (topping a pair of silky combat pants). A little bit of stretch means it will retain its shape on business trips, and luxe materials will elevate even jeans. Finally, avoid details that are likely to date. You should be spending as much as you can afford, so the least you can expect is longevity.

THE FINER POINTS, PART 2

Three pairs of pants or three skirts should be enough for starters. You're aiming for quality rather than quantity. Save the throwaway fashion statements for weekends. Above the waist, five tops to every skirt or pair of pants you own is plenty. Thankfully, these don't require breaking the bank. Mid-tier labels are an excellent source, and even mass-market T-shirts are fine, provided they are pristine. The same goes for knitwear. (It's smart practice to keep a lint brush in your desk drawer.) If button-up shirts seem too masculine, consider medium-to-heavy-weight silk blouses that will look good with or without a jacket. They're worth the outlay, as much for the feminine details as for the fit.

Once you've got the pieces in place, mixing textures is an effective way to achieve a balance of formal and modern. Try, for instance, a tweed jacket with velvet pants or a leather bomber jacket with gabardine pants. They can look exceedingly smart without falling into the deathly trap of boring corporatism.

GOING THE EXTRA MILE

In the land of corner offices, status symbols represent power. That Louis Vuitton bag might actually be a career investment. Actually, top-notch accessories are always worth prioritizing, particularly bags. There are some good inexpensive shoes around, but it's much harder to score a beautiful cheap bag. On the other hand, don't bankrupt yourself. If good leather is too pricey, consider a dark canvas or nylon alternative. If it's your first job, no one will expect you to be dripping in prestige labels. In fact, if you are, you could send the wrong message.

In the land of corner offices, status symbols represent power. That Louis Vuitton bag might actually be a career investment.

Accessories also smooth the day-to-night transformation that's inevitable in a working woman's life. You may want to slip some lacy hose and fun costume jewelry next to that defuzzer for those days. Shoes, like perhaps a jeweled sandal, are another instant look changer. Rationalize, strategize, streamline. It could work for more than just your office style.

WELL SUITED

• THE LIGHTER SIDE

The suit might be less common these days, but it's still a sharp-looking boardroom staple. However, now the set piece has become more fluid in its once starched and rigid parameters. Look for modern versions that break the rules with short sleeves, softly structured jackets and stylish mismatching.

• FINISH WITH EDGE

There's a certain level of formality and authority that comes along with a suit—and those are important elements. After all, power dressing exists for a reason. Therefore it's up to your accessories to inject some air into the proceedings. Try a neutral strappy sandal instead of a classic pump or a sleek and bright bag.

• THE TROMPE L'OEIL SUIT

Question: When is a suit not a suit? Answer: When you've successfully assembled a group of crisp tailored pieces in a harmonious composition to read in a suitlike manner. One good tip: Don't worry about exact matches, work tonally.

Desiree
Rogers

Marion
Cotillard

Kathryn
Bigelow

Lighten up the power surge of a suit with a bold but bright necklace, a coolly architectural sandal or a laid-back-but-luxe classic watch.

POLISHED PIECES

• GOING THE DISTANCE

It's true, the dress has one-step ease. However, when you're building a work wardrobe that has to withstand the daily grind without requiring an astronomical clothing budget, smart separates that can be mixed and matched in endless variations are a savvier choice.

• CLASSIC WITH A TWIST

It's a cliché expression, but for great office style it's wholly appropriate. Even creative jobs require a degree of professionalism where your wardrobe isn't a distraction. Keep your twists subtle, like an A-line skirt cut in dark leather with a hint of sheen or tailored trousers in an unexpected bright hue.

• COMFORT EQUALS CONFIDENCE

Pairing dark jeans with a tailored jacket is always an appropriate way to bring casual ease to office wear, but you can achieve the same easy feel sans denim by selecting fluid trousers, soft knits and silk blouses.

Pull together skirts, blouses and pants
with extras that are stylishly serious,
like a lace-up oxford, masculine-inspired
clutch or leather-bound notebooks.

95

DAY TO NIGHT DRESSES

- **ROCK AROUND THE CLOCK**

  Twenty-four-hour careers leave scant time to run home and change. Thankfully, the humble dress offers a direct solution. Toeing the professional/party time divide, however, can be delicate. Opt for simplicity and generally clean lines with just a hint of detail—no feathers or undulating ruffles.

- **HUE RESOURCES**

  A nice dose of solid color is also a good way to bridge the two spheres. Steer away from anything overly eye-popping. Instead of brights, think intense and rich shades.

- **JUST ADD A JACKET**

  The easiest way to make a dress look right for nine-to-five is to top it off with a tailored jacket. Investing in a beautiful sharp black blazer can turn entire swaths of your wardrobe that were previously off-limits office-appropriate. When it's time to go out, just remove said jacket.

Jemima Khan

Carolina Herrera

Rachel
Weisz

January
Jones

Elettra
Wiedemann

Transforming a dress from career
woman to cocktail can be a matter
of small changes, like adding a
bejeweled sandal, a metallic handbag
or a chunky cocktail ring.

97

CHAPTER 5

OFF-DUTY CHIC

Beyond the office dress code,
personal style takes flight

A CASUAL AFFAIR

There's a whole wide world of fashion
to be explored out of the office.
The one thing that's out-of-bounds?
Messy looks and clothes that have passed
their freshness date. Once you nail
down the basics, you'll be ready
to relax in style without working
too hard on deciding what to wear.

THE WEEKENDS ARE NO REASON NOT TO LOOK TERRIFIC.
Since you are liberated from office codes and constraints, this should be your moment. The first step to acquiring that enviable air that the truly stylish exude is to feel relaxed. While you should certainly have fun trying out various trends, this may not be the time for flamboyant fashion statements. It's far better to project the image of someone who is happy in her own skin (and style).

THE COAT THAT HAS YOU COVERED

Creating an ensemble intended to be worn when you're not working shouldn't be, well, work. Enter the trench coat. It's one of the hardest-working pieces in your wardrobe. On those off-duty days, it covers a multitude of sins by lending a sharper and more pulled-together feel to whatever you might be wearing. No wonder it's a part of iconic fashion moments like the one pictured here with Catherine Deneuve on the set of *The Umbrellas of Cherbourg*.

Our heroine of the hour is Brigitte Bardot, on holiday in the beloved fishing port (as it then was) of Saint-Tropez. Her wardrobe of flat sandals, unpretentious cotton sundresses and white jeans wasn't necessarily expensive, but it was all beautifully cut and perfect for her. Fast-forward a few decades, and Phoebe Philo, the creative director of Céline, is another woman who knows about the unspoken power of hand-picked separates when it comes to creating an aura of effortless chic.

DAYS OF CALM, BUT NOT CARELESSNESS

It may be that you already have the basic template for weekend style and all you need for day-of-rest perfection is to upgrade existing pieces. The difference between an ill-crafted T-shirt and a perfect stripy tee is like comparing boxed merlot and Château Lafite. Both are red wine; one is infinitely better. The fact that your denim and V-neck sweater aren't cocktail attire is not the problem. It's that the knit is irreparably pilled and those jeans are so baggy, they seem to add 15 pounds to your frame.

Yet for many women, weekends are for clothes that have been relegated. Too old, too faded or just past their prime, these pieces get filtered down through the closet until they reach the weekend section, where they sit like unwanted sediment. That's no way to go about boosting anyone's confidence or sense of style. Yet most of us are guilty of accepting this so-called system, whether it's out of a misplaced sense of guilt or because we were raised on outdated notions about keeping our best clothes for those "best" occasions. According to this skewed logic, a laid-back Saturday afternoon isn't one of those moments. But even if you spend most of your off-duty time where you're unlikely to see anyone you need to impress, there's still value in looking your best.

The difference between an ill-crafted T-SHIRT and a perfect STRIPY TEE is like comparing boxed merlot and Château Lafite. Both are red wine; one is INFINITELY BETTER.

THE STAR SYSTEM

The first step in nailing off-duty style is to determine unflinchingly what it is we actually spend most of our off hours doing. Many of us err in buying for a fantasy life, and those purchases inevitably add to the sediment. Once you've eliminated all the dross, you can replace it with a less-is-more capsule

 I think personal style starts from within because it's a philosophy and an attitude. If you're honest and true to yourself, you will have the best sense of personal style. If you try and be someone else, it will never work because it's always very transparent when somebody is trying to mimic someone else. Less is always more with personal style. Just know yourself, know what works for you and be naturally confident in expressing that.

—STELLA MCCARTNEY

of star performers. There's no point in putting up with anything that makes us feel less than on top of our game. The so-sos should be bagged up and given away to charity. An important distinction while separating sartorial wheat from chaff: Worn in is not the same as worn-out. Assembling a first-rate cast of weekend performers needn't be exorbitant. Labels such as Gap and J. Crew have truly come into their own for these pieces. Conversely, while designer jeans can seem expensive, they go far. Their cost per wear (and per impact) should work out in cents rather than dollars.

SATURDAYS IN THE CITY

If your weekends are mainly spent in the city with friends, either visiting galleries, lunching or shopping, then along with the ultimate pair of jeans and half a dozen immaculate T-shirts (you don't need more; simply replace them when they begin to gray or bag), you'll probably want a jacket that strikes a balance. A tailored blazer oozes dressed-down chic when it's in jersey, corduroy or cotton velvet. And don't count out the wonders

If your weekends are about hunkering down in the country, then cozy should be your benchmark. This is not to be confused with sloppy.

of a lightweight tweed. It's a hardy fabric that's infinitely versatile, not least because most tweeds are composed of a myriad of different colors that make them easy to accessorize. A thick knit sweater coat or jacket also does the trick but has a softer ease to it. These aren't cheap, but a good one has longevity.

If you love jeans but don't always want to wear denim, look for all the other fabrications on offer, like corduroy, cotton and canvas. You may also want two or three dresses, like shirtwaists and tunics, in easy-care fine cottons, which are a fabulous option that can be layered over thick tights in the winter or with jeans for a flattering go-anywhere look. Unless you're someone who doesn't mind making endless detours to the dry cleaner (and paying those stealthily steep bills), it's a good idea to keep weekend clothes as low maintenance as possible. When it comes to knitwear, choose wisely and don't scrimp; these are pieces you can wear to work as well. As for outerwear, it's hard to beat a peacoat or a trench coat for understated chic.

SUNDAYS IN THE COUNTRY

If your weekends are about hunkering down in the country, then cozy should be your benchmark. This is not to be confused with sloppy. Elasticized waists, borrowed items from your gym bag and trouser shapes that haven't been fashionable for five years are all inadmissible. Saggy is not the same thing as boyfriend cut. One has been designed to hang beautifully and is artfully oversized. The other resembles a sack. By all means exercise your right to comfort, but elevate this to an art with luxurious, quietly glamorous fabrics: washed silks, fine cottons, chambrays and cheesecloths. Some of these are purposefully made to look better wrinkled.

If you love sheepskin boots, consider instead a pair with a leather exterior, as they can look more sophisticated while providing that same delicious, squishy feeling. If you need a practical workhorse of a coat, a down-filled parka is hard to beat. Recently, there have been some knockout budget versions. (Check out Uniqlo, where Jil Sander has been working her magic.)

THE FINAL WORD

Pulling all of the above together requires luxurious but understated indulgences, like a gorgeous cashmere scarf or a beautiful belt. (A caramel leather is lovely, as is something woven.) A fine gold or silver chain with a precious little pendant peeking out from a T-shirt can take your basics beyond. Then, a practical but cool medium to small-sized bag that can slip over the shoulders or strap across the body is the kind of micropleasure that can't be underestimated.

CITY CHIC

• BEYOND BASIC

It's a fashion truth you'll
hear repeatedly: All dressed-
down clothes are not
created equal. A great off-duty
look is built around at least
one beautifully made and
considered piece—a perfect
cashmere sweatshirt, a gorgeous tweed coat or a luxurious
accessory—that makes all its
laid-back companion items
snap to attention.

• OVER AND OVER

Layering is an essential element
when it comes to casual
style and clothes that might
potentially serve a few pur-
poses. After all, a day off could
mean anything from errands
to early cocktails. But limit
yourself to two or three (layers,
that is, not cocktails). Anything
more quickly turns messy.

• HEEL CAREFULLY

The flip side to a slapdash
appearance is trying too
hard to maintain a glamorous
look when glamour isn't
called for. So when it comes to
shoes, find a solid boot in
which you can pound the
pavement, and leave the sky-
high platforms at home.

Gwyneth
Paltrow

Anja
Rubik

Diane
Kruger

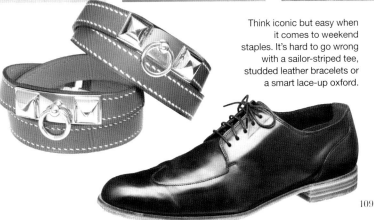

Think iconic but easy when it comes to weekend staples. It's hard to go wrong with a sailor-striped tee, studded leather bracelets or a smart lace-up oxford.

COUNTRY CASUAL

• RELAX, LOOK CHIC

The good news about dressing
for weekends spent far from
the bustle of city life is that
many labels now offer exactly
what you need: cozy but
well-crafted knits, pants that
borrow that ease of sweats
sans the ick factor and utili-
tarian-influenced coats that are
both warm and stylish.

• INNER BEAUTY

Don't forget about the essentials that aren't outwardly visible
to others when you're off in
the chilly hinterlands. Having
at your disposal a selection of
silk and cotton undershirts and
woolen tights to wear under
clothes can make all the difference between fun and freezing.

• ROOM FOR ROMANCE

There's a necessary hardiness
to country gear, but every now
and then you might think about
channeling the aristocratic
charm of an English manor
by adding to the mix a chiffon
dress, layered of course with a
chunky sweater and stockings.

Country weekend pieces aren't about the latest It item. A smart satchel, a tweed blazer and a rugged but refined ankle boot are just right.

GREAT COATS

• OUTER SPACE

Outerwear multitasks. You can wear the same trench to a Monday board meeting as you do to Sunday brunch. But solidly stylish toppers are an intrinsic part of a casual wardrobe. If you make it your goal to buy one classic, high-quality coat every year, you should be able to build a strong collection that fills any cover-up need and lasts many years.

• THE CHECKLIST

Wants are different from needs, which in turn are distinct from ideals. So, which coats should you ideally have in a complete wardrobe? A long wool or tweed overcoat, a peacoat or waist-length car coat, a down coat either in place of or in addition to a shearling or fur for deep winter, a chic anorak or something stylish yet sporty and, last but not least, a trench.

Finish the look with a jaunty hat, a luxuriously sizable cashmere scarf and even colorful gloves—like this pair identical to those Michelle Obama wore on inauguration day.

JEAN THERAPY

• NEUTRAL STATES

Jeans might be indigo, but like black or beige, they go with literally everything. That makes the humble blue jean ideal when you're nurturing personal style. In many ways, it's a blank slate to make your own in whichever direction you'd like to go.

• CORRECT CUT, COLOR

The denim market is a deep, deep blue sea, with literally something for everyone, no matter your requirements. The abundant choices can also lead to confusion if you don't happen to know what your requirements should be.

Do your homework by spending a quality hour or so at a department store with a comprehensive selection, trying on as many pairs as possible. You'll soon learn invaluable information about what works for you.

• IN THE MIX

Denim is a crucial part of the high-low mélange that is now part of modern dressing. Pairing your jeans with anything ostentatious or expensive immediately turns down the volume on said piece. Et voilà: a look that hits casual chic squarely on the mark.

Rachel Bilson

Stella McCartney

Kate
Moss

Gaia
Repossi

Sienna
Miller

Denim partners beautifully
with nearly any accessory,
from a bold animal-print bag
to an industrially crafty
bracelet and a classic buckled
leather boot.

THE EASY DRESS

• LIKE ABC, 123

What could be more casual than an item of clothing that completes a look in essentially one step? Of course, we're not talking about a razor-slim shift but rather a floaty frock that's ease incarnate. Silhouettes that are nipped gently at the waist with a slightly full or flared skirt can do no wrong.

• PATTERN FORMING

Have fun with prints and patterns when you're looking for off-duty dresses. There are endless varieties of florals alone to explore, not to mention abstracts, stripes and plaids.

• BREEZY, NOT BUSY

Resist the urge to clutter your dress with accessories. A lovely dress is a statement in itself. Why complicate it? Just add a sandal, ballet flat or comfy wedge, choose between a belt and a bauble and go.

Minnie
Mortimer-Gaghan

Isabel
Lucas

Christy
Turlington

Keep your sunny-day dress
effortless by choosing
one or two extras
with personality, like
retro-cool sunglasses,
sophisticated flat sandals
or a tie-dyed bag.

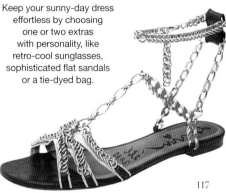

117

CHAPTER 6

EVENING GLAMOUR

A special occasion becomes
something to celebrate
when you've got the
perfect party ensemble

THE SOCIAL CALL

Putting on a party dress isn't something
we do every day. As a result, it can
send even the most stylish of women
into a turmoil about what to wear.
But that elusive perfect evening
ensemble isn't out of anyone's grasp.
It just takes a little groundwork.

ARTY. ONE SMALL, INNOCUOUS WORD, ONE BIG TAILSPIN.
With the celebratory implications come high expectations of
what to wear. Interpretations of festive dress vary enormously
depending on whether the event in question is a wedding,
birthday, anniversary, black-tie event or cocktail party. That's
before we get down to location—city, country, beach—which
makes a tremendous difference to the tone of an occasion.

One of Truman Capote's social "swans," Babe Paley, was known for her singular style, which was by turns elegant, effortless and always her own. On the night of Dwight D. Eisenhower's inaugural ball, Paley more than met the high expectations of the evening in a boldly dramatic gown and jeweled collar. Almost sixty years later, it's still a vision to behold.

"For me, Queen Rania of Jordan perfectly embodies what it means to have personal style. She is beautiful, of course, with a model-like physique, and she carries herself regally like the queen she is, but it goes beyond that [because] style is more than just clothes. It is the way Queen Rania lives her life, balancing her official duties with raising a family of four children and her deep involvement in philanthropic work. She blends tradition with modernism for an exquisite fit in all.

—GIORGIO ARMANI "

The primary guideline is, of course, your invitation, which should specify the level of formality. But beyond that, navigating a special-occasion ensemble can often throw up many roadblocks.

YOU ARE INVITED...TO SHOP EARLY

However rarely you're required to dress up, it pays to be prepared. A specific event provides an excellent bona fide excuse to buy something new, but there's nothing like an imminent deadline to muddle the brain and miraculously empty the stores of anything remotely suitable. A tightly edited festive repertoire prevents impulse purchases. It's worth investing as much as you can afford. Trends come and go, but for parties, they tend to sit tight. Provided you avoid details with obvious built-in obsolescence (big shoulders, asymmetric necklines, ultra-short hems, puffballs, exaggerated flares,) they'll last for years.

Classics are classics for a reason. A choice among the little black, little navy-blue or little gray dress is your passport to most formal

Classics are classics for a reason. A choice among the little black, little navy-blue or little gray dress is your passport to most formal events.

events. For day, including weddings, just take the color down a few shades. Shine casts a flattering glow on the face, but it also draws the eye to lumps and bumps. It's better to use pearls, diamonds, diamanté or a huge jeweled neck plate to light up your skin. While brocades and patterns have instant appeal, they can become all too familiar after a few outings. This staple of a dress should fit beautifully. If necessary, get it altered. It may underwhelm on the hanger, but on the body great tailoring has all the kick of Tabasco and will stand you in better stead than surface embellishment.

THE LONG, SHORT AND OTHERWISE

While a floor-length dress remains the ultimate indicator of formality, showing off gleaming skin is still a party signifier. To a degree, the rule seems to be the skimpier the dress, the more festive. Necklines have plunged at night since the sixteenth century. That's still no excuse for vulgarity. Bare arms, legs and back (within reason) always look classier than cleavage as deep as the Grand Canyon.

Sometimes, only a long dress will do. If the hostess stipulates floor length, it takes a brave soul to rebel. While cheap evening wear isn't easy to find, there are now lots of labels in the market just below designer that do a terrific job. Also worth investigating are some of the new dress-rental services that have started to pop up. Going the vintage route is another tempting solution. Even if you're not habitually drawn to retro styles, the luxurious fabrics, painstaking workmanship and classic shapes all work beautifully at night and for a fraction of the cost of a new dress. Should you find yourself in love with something so formal it involves a train, corset or pouf, make sure it won't wreck your evening by impeding you or anyone else.

Conversely, if the idea of wearing long makes you squirm, you have two options. The first is to find a short dress so deliciously dramatic that no one focuses on its length. The second is to hunt down a simply styled long dress in a laid-back fabric like cotton jersey or washed silk. Wear it with flat jeweled sandals and you'll look perfect at beach weddings and

Penelope
Tree

DRESS THIS WAY,
S'IL VOUS PLAIT

Truman Capote's Black and White Ball in 1966 was a high point for interpreting party-attire instruction. Guests, like a 17-year-old Penelope Tree, pictured at left, were asked to come in only black and white, and of course a mask. To make invitation jargon fun rather than frustrating, here's your guide.

• FESTIVE: Mostly used around the holidays, this term connotes a degree of flexibility in formality and welcomes boldly jubilant touches like bright colors, sparkle and ruffles.

• COCKTAIL: Common and classic, cocktail allows anything from elegant work wear, sufficiently kicked up with jewels and heels, to a proper knee-length cocktail frock, such as your staple LBD. Syn.: semiformal.

• BLACK TIE: Where once the starchily formal term meant that only a floor-length gown would do, now a luxuriously stylish knee-length dress can be appropriate. One rule of thumb: Imagine yourself on the arm of a tuxedo-clad man and make sure you're not going so casual as to appear mismatched. Syn.: formal.

• WHITE TIE: The apex of formality, a white-tie affair requires a floor-length gown, whether it's a column or a full ball-skirted look. Accoutrements like gloves and a wrap for the shoulders are optional, but if you're feeling fancy, why not? Syn.: full evening dress.

125

glamorous poolside lunches. Having a long dress that you love in your closet will stop you from rushing out and splurging on an awful one through blind panic. Choose carefully, and you'll have it for life. You may not wear it often, but like the go-anywhere black lace top, it's like money in the bank.

BEYOND THE FROCK

If a dress seems too predictable, consider a tuxedo suit. This classic has never quite lost its status as the genteel rebel choice and will take you anywhere from a smart dinner to the Oscars. When done properly (for lessons, see Charlotte Rampling and other European femmes fatales), it's devastatingly seductive, and not merely because nothing becomes a woman so well as looking as if she hasn't tried too hard.

Under the sexy lighting of an evening event, rhinestones and diamanté can have the same impact as the real thing.

A beautiful duchess satin, silk crepe or sequin skirt with a fabulously dramatic blouse is another versatile solution. Like a tuxedo, this pairing can be sexy and sharp while only minimally revealing. As a general rule, the more formal the occasion, the wispier the top you wear. The right cut on a tuxedo jacket can help you get away with wearing nothing underneath apart from a drop-dead-gorgeous bra. (Never ever scrimp on lingerie, especially at night.) Don't forget to schedule a trip to the hair salon. If you're going understated, you need to play up your natural assets. It's a basic formula for a killer look that's guaranteed to quietly steal the show.

THE ICING ON THE COCKTAIL CAKE

What you add to an understated dress is crucial. A capsule selection of party shoes can include one metallic pair that goes with everything and one in satin or velvet. Then you can have fun with chandelier earrings and little evening bags (jeweled, shiny, tasseled or dripping in marabou). Unlike your dress, these don't need to be investments. Have fun digging up costume jewelry and little beaded pochettes from the flea market or vintage shop. Under the sexy lighting of an evening event, rhinestones and diamanté can have the same impact as the real thing.

Then there's the question of what to wear over your dress. Some of the hippest partygoers these days wear their Moncler quilted jackets over their duchess-satin ball gowns for that goddess-goes-sporty-urban look. A beaded vest, jewel-encrusted cardigan or embroidered cashmere shawl can have the same effect when it comes to making a formal outfit seem more youthful. The silhouette should complement your dress. A classically shaped silk trench is a chic option that works over dresses that are the same length or slightly longer. The most versatile shape is a boxy, hip-length jacket that's long enough to keep you warm but short enough to work with any length dress, or even trousers.

By the way, this is where you can be crafty with your money: You want something that will make an impact, but you'll probably remove it the moment you arrive. The rest of the time, it will exist in darkness. So by all means go for a fun, high-drama choice from a high-fashion chain. Feathers, velvet, sequins and sparkly tweed are all reliable showstoppers.

COCKTAIL HOUR

• BLACK, NOT BASIC

The LBD is an evergreen choice, but your go-to party dress could be navy, gray or even nude. Nevertheless, don't let the sensible nature of the color sway you into selecting a silhouette that's humdrum. Instead look for a dress with subtle details like lace trim, panels, embroidery or pleating.

• BUT IF YOU DO COLOR...

Think of intense hues as a design element in and of themselves. Wear a dress in a rich jewel tone or a beautiful bright and you really need little else. The color says it all. Of course, it won't go under the radar as easily as a neutral frock that easily bears frequent wears, but if you buy a winner—with an ultraflattering shade and cut—it can last you for years.

• END IT WELL

Not the night, but rather your look. It's easy to get wrapped up in The Dress, but also be sure you have the right accessories—especially shoes. Don't ruin an evening look with ill-matched casual footwear.

Leigh Lezark

Aerin Lauder

Naomi
Watts

Julianne
Moore

Demi
Moore

With a colorful cocktail ring,
exquisite little clutch
and satin sandals, even
a simple dress can achieve
after-eight perfection.

129

BIG NIGHT

• THE LONG WAY

A black-tie event usually requires a long dress, but that's a pretty vast category. Consider practical concerns in your choice. If you want to end the evening on the dance floor, for example, don't go for a train, no matter how much you love the gown.

• RED-CARPET TUTORIAL

You're not placing your gown under the glaring scrutiny of the media gauntlet at the Oscars, but adopting some of those awards-show pros' best practices isn't a bad idea. First, do a trial run in your dress and make sure that you can walk without snagging your heels or being too constricted. If your event is a well-photographed affair—like a wedding—snap a few pics to see how it reads on film.

• LOOK, MA, NO STRAPS

Strapless gowns can be a supremely elegant statement, but not if they don't fit and look as if they're going to slip off. Visit a tailor beforehand to avoid that regrettable fate.

Poppy
Delevigne

Natalie
Portman

Maggie
Gyllenhaal

Iman

Rachel
Roy

A beautiful gown
doesn't need much
help, but one beautiful
piece of jewelry
and a dazzling pair
of shoes make a
winning finish.

131

THE DRESS ALTERNATIVE

• TROUSER PRESS

A beautiful dress can make your night, but there's a certain swaggering freedom in taking a page from the menswear book for a special occasion every now and then.

• AT THE TUXEDO JUNCTION

Granted, that sharply cut black satin tuxedo is timeless. There are, in fact, a few options beyond a dress or a skirt for evening. Simply flip the coin on that tux and try it in white, or choose a suit in a party-time color like red or silvery gray, and add appropriately festive accessories. Or lose the jacket and just tuck an exquisite blouse into tailored trousers and be done.

• A FINAL FEMININE TOUCH

Take a light hand with your borrowed-from-the-boys inspiration. Keep accessories sleek but still very ladylike with a touch of glamour.

Penélope
Cruz

Emily
Blunt

Melanie
Laurent

Add some flash to
your menswear-inspired
evening with a
chunky bejeweled
cuff or a metallic bag.

GREAT COVER-UPS

• TOP THIS

There are two equally valid schools of thought on the evening topper. The first: Choose a coat that's over-the-top and arrive in dramatic fashion. After all, why not have fun with a stunning piece that makes only a cameo appearance? The second: Keep your after-eight outerwear elegantly discreet so that when you remove it, jaws drop at the magnificence underneath.

• ALL NIGHT LONG

Some cover-ups aren't just for warmth. A beautiful brocade blazer or a luxurious fur vest can give youthful edge to your old cocktail frock. Don't banish these to the coat check.

• PROTECTION PROGRAM

If you don't have the perfect topper, it's still no reason to brave the elements in only your gown (unless, of course, it's undeniably balmy). Even if you're just wearing your classic trench—a perfectly respectable choice—a beautiful dress requires a little protection in transit.

Vanessa
Paradis

Tilda
Swinton

Sarah
Jessica
Parker

A fanciful cuff or a beaded lariat
is elegant when peeking out
from a coat, while a long chain
evening bag slings jauntily
over any topper.

135

JEWELRY AND MORE

• TO STAR OR SUPPORT?

Despite the connotation as an extra element, accessories can be both leading ladies and supporting players. Much like the stage, both are potentially pivotal roles. On Amy Adams, a multicolored bib necklace stole the red carpet show with a big and bold statement. Meanwhile, Angelina Jolie's gorgeous emerald teardrop earrings lent precise and subtle sizzle to her low-key black gown. If you're wearing delicate jewels, it's okay to wear a few pieces, but sometimes one breathtaking dazzler is all you need.

• SHINE, HIGH AND LOW

Evening looks are about bringing light, and maybe a little magic, to the night. So while diamonds might be a girl's pro-verbial best friend, rhinestones and other faux bling on cos-tume jewelry and even shoes and handbags are the smartest way to get that glow.

Amy Adams

Angelina Jolie

LITTLE
TREASURES
like these are the key
to evening looks
with personality.

CHAPTER 7

ESSENTIAL EXTRAS

Great style is in the bag...
and the shoe
and the silk scarf.
The right accessories
are crucial.

A FLOURISH THAT FINISHES

Accessories are often an afterthought, but a mere bag, belt or brooch can be the difference between a look that sings and one that's just so-so. Investing some time and effort into assembling a wardrobe of perfect pieces is a smart strategy for the long haul.

WOMAN'S BEST ACCESSORY WILL ALWAYS BE her mind. That said, who couldn't use a little help to pep things up every now and then? If clothes are the foundation of style, accessories are the moldings, the shutters and the filigree. Even the most dedicated minimalist can make her point more emphatically with one exquisitely chosen ring (now *that's* a statement) than with nothing at all (which can easily look like an oversight).

SMALL DETAILS IN THE BIG PICTURE

While you wouldn't leave home shoeless or without your handbag, you might forget that special little touch with high impact, like sixties style icon Marianne Faithfull's oversized sunglasses pictured here. Indeed, this iconic image might be less so without the cartoony cool of Faithfull's striped frames. Clothes may get the lion's share of glory, but that extra, sometimes unexpected, twist can make all the difference.

In recent years, fashion has caught up with the allure of accessories. First came the It bag, then the It necklace, the It cuff, the It shoe. The self-parodying culture of It has at least reminded us that accessories aren't just the optional icing on top.

THE ABC'S OF ACCESSORIES

Assembling a closet of accessories can seem daunting and expensive, but the task doesn't have to be either. For sure, money will change hands, but a gold cuff you wear every day for a year, put away for two, then bring out again for the next twenty constitutes a sound investment even by your bank manager's steely standards. Besides, accessories don't always have to be pricey. By all means splurge on a good watch, but also educate your eye by scrutinizing the windows of Harry Winston or the high-end costume jewelry at Lanvin

By all means splurge on a good watch, but also educate your eye by scrutinizing the windows of Harry Winston or the high-end costume jewelry at Lanvin and Dior.

and Dior. Then endlessly scour flea markets, ethnic stalls and the racks in H&M, all of which can yield the most gratifying treasures.

There's an almost artistic nature to incorporating these fantastic finds. Necklines and waistlines can be nipped and tucked with the judicious pinning of a brooch or the firm tightening of a belt. The nonchalant tossing on of several yards of pearls or chunky chains can lengthen a neck while looking like liquid armor. Coco Chanel was right about elegance being refusal (read: Don't clutter yourself like a Christmas tree), but she more

MAKE A STATEMENT
with shoes that are
everything but ordinary.

than anyone, apart from Coco Chanel, knew that quantity is not the problem, but groupings are. When it comes to jewels, most women look better when they concentrate on one area. Wear a tower of bangles up one arm, for instance, but not a simultaneous lasso of necklaces and tangle of earrings. Then again, some women, like Loulou de la Falaise, look fabulous doing just that. With accessories, it's not sticking to the rules that counts so much as how you break them.

 What's personal style? It's first of all about knowing yourself. Being individual in your choices. Being obsessive. Having strong takes on things. It's a gesture, a way to speak, a choice of words, a way to move. It's an allure in the French meaning.

—BRUNO FRISONI,
CREATIVE DIRECTOR,
ROGER VIVIER

A STAR IS BORN

Sometimes an accessory is the crux of an outfit. Just consider Lanvin's crystal-smothered neck plates (just add a T-shirt and you *shall* go to the ball) or Miuccia Prada's personal collection of antique diamonds (no mistaking her for a librarian with those beauties twinkling by her jawline). That's especially true if you're striving for a timeless, chic simplicity with your clothes. Look at Angelina Jolie's black sheath dress at the Academy Awards ceremony in 2009. Her beautiful but stark statement became unforgettable when she added those emerald drop earrings. Similarly, a wicked pair of zebra-print Alaïa gladiator sandals can act like a blood transfusion for your five-year-old black linen shift dress. Chances are, if you fall in love with a beautiful pair of shoes or a cocktail ring that borders on being a work of art, it can be a game changer in your wardrobe and a cornerstone around which to build entire looks.

THE SUPPORTING CAST

A closet spilling over with headlining accessories isn't necessarily the gift from heaven it seems if it doesn't have the essentials. To start, a pair of patent pumps are an eternally smart and low-maintenance option. Also tick off on your list canvas sneakers for weekends, biker boots for pants and shorter skirts, knee-high boots for smart skirts and high-heeled sandals for summertime polish and the occasional wintertime wearing with tights.

As for flat sandals, unless you choose the pair that's on every billboard, these tend not to date much. Jackie O–esque leather thongs have been in fashion for four decades. But

For the nighttime necessities, you may unleash your inner siren. I'm talking about high heels and velvet, satin, silk, lace, vivid color and embellishment.

remember, one stand-out pair will do more than half a dozen mediocrities. That's also sound advice for your everyday handbag, which should be a couple of pounds of buttery leather that simply lifts your spirits to look at and wear. Of all your fashion purchases, you'll be using it more than anything. Take care (and probably some cash) in choosing the right one.

Also necessary, but often forgotten, is assembling a belt wardrobe that runs the gamut of thin, wide, patent, rugged and metallic. They're the purchases that may seem inconsequential at the time but crucial when you find yourself in need of the right one.

For the nighttime necessities, you may unleash your inner siren. I'm talking about high heels and velvet, satin, silk, lace, vivid color and embellishment. This is not the moment to consult your podiatrist but a chance to indulge your senses. A beautiful pair of evening shoes hardly ever dates. They'll be worth every cent. For evenings bags: See the above. While we're on the subject of flash, every woman needs some glittering rocks in her life—or failing that, some cubic zirconia. Bold but fake is almost always better than prissy but real.

DASHES OF DARING

Bad taste is the grit in the fashion oyster that ends up producing the pearl. Knowing when to inject that vital shot of vulgarity is what sorts the bland from the stylish, the predictable from the head turning. Love leopard print but not a whole coat's worth? Yearn for a touch of red? This is where scarves, bags, belts, gloves and even sunglasses come in. The days of discreet coordination are long past, and while an alligator bag or crocodile belt remain a timeless beacon of desirability, nowadays for that youthful joie de vivre a woman needs her accessories to be more than passive status symbols. Whitney Port's pastel-pink sunglasses lifted her airport ensemble of gray sweatshirt and white chinos from perfectly okay to adorably and effortlessly kooky. Get accessories right and they'll make you feel powerful as well as chic.

THE SHOE CLOSET

• A FOOTWEAR FOUNDATION

Shoes set the tone of a look. Therefore it's good practice to build a core collection that covers the range of your needs. Start with smart ballet flat, a patent pump, a neutral heel, a comfortable but chic wedge and a day-to-night sandal.

• BLUR THE LINES

There's no need to stay within old-school parameters of which shoe is appropriate when and where. You might not have originally thought of those beige pumps as an evening option, but they might just look great with a cocktail dress.

• SHOP WITH CARE

You could be wearing the most beautiful shoes in the world, but if you can't walk in them, there's no chance of knocking 'em dead. Buying shoes requires a deeper level of scrutiny than clothes. Give them a test run both in the store and on carpeting at home (so as not to scuff the soles if a return is in order) to ensure proper fit and comfort.

Carey Mulligan

Camilla Belle

BOOT CAMP

• SECURITY MEETS STYLE

Even if they're on a treacherously high heel, boots have a certain hardy quality. They offer coverage, protection and in many cases comfort. In short, one or two or even three various pairs should be a part of your footwear repertoire.

• START HIGH AND LOW

Your basic boot set should ideally include one ankle boot and another that hovers around the knee, whether slightly under or over. A high-heeled ankle boot works beautifully with trousers, jeans and flared skirts, while a knee boot is a perfect partner to all kinds of skirts, dresses and skinny jeans.

• THE DAILY SHOW

During fall and winter, a great boot can be your go-to footwear. A flat is always a smart option, but also consider one with a wedge or a sturdy block heel that won't hinder being on the go for both work and weekends. Unless you're facing down half a foot of snow, one choice pair can get you through the chillier months, fitting your needs for both function and flash.

Gisele Bündchen

Mary-Kate Olsen

BEST BAGS

• AN EVERYDAY AFFAIR

Put thought into selecting the bag you'll be toting around every day. Think three parts practicality to one part fantasy. Luxe satchels and larger frame bags fit the bill nicely. Since they're a no-brainer to match, brown and black are logical color choices, but hues like bright red, oxblood and navy also mix well with day-to-day looks.

• SMALL WONDERS

Diminutive bags, like oversized wallets and evening clutches, are a chance to have a little fun with embellishment, exotic skins and metallics—styles that might not be your daily go-tos. Everything works in small doses.

• THE IT FACTOR

Handbags are susceptible to hyper-popularity and It-ness, which have a way of making you feel that you simply must have them. That's not to say you shouldn't buy the bag of the moment. Most deserve the mantle. Just consider carefully: Will you still love it when the fashion furor dies down?

Alexa Chung

Charlize Theron

SCARVES AND BELTS

• TIE ONE ON (AND ON)

A quality collection of scarves and belts is built over time. These are things that don't spoil when the season's done. One new annual addition of each is enough to amass what you need. The trick is remembering to buy them *before* you're in dire need of that extra kick.

• TRY THIS AT HOME

Incorporating a belt isn't always easy. Take time to experiment. Cinch a cardigan over a floaty frock with a skinny belt or unite a skirt and blouse with a wide cummerbund-esque piece. Or use one to maximize your proportions: to carve a sleek hourglass on a curvy figure or to create shape on a boyish frame.

• THE WRAP STAR

Scarves have nearly endless possibility. Printed silk can simply be draped over the shoulder or knotted at the neck with a jacket or cardigan. Colorful cashmere is a bright way to stay warm in fall and spring with a light jacket, while long gauzy cotton versions are summer styling essentials.

Carla Bruni-Sarkozy

Kate Bosworth

Tory
Burch

Fabiola
Beracasa

Margherita
Missoni

Give smart pieces, like
a chic fur vest, even more
snap with a beautiful belt or
a colorful scarf.

155

CHAPTER 8

THE GETAWAY

From the beach to the mountains and back again, traveling fashionably can be a breeze

STYLE TAKES NO HOLIDAY

Going on a vacation can test both the strength of your wardrobe and your commitment to fashion over comfort. With some sage advice about dressing and packing you'll pass with flying colors.

RAVEL HAS GIVEN US SOME TRULY ICONIC MOMENTS. Just think of Brigitte Bardot frolicking by the ocean in her teeny bikini and Ali McGraw racing out of the airport with Steve McQueen in an effortlessly chic scoop-neck T-shirt and belled trousers. Perhaps that's why it's doubly disappointing that vacationers often let their wardrobe standards flag.

THE SIMPLE LIFE

Whether it's to Tuscany or Tortola, a vacation is about escaping everyday complications. That's why the strategy of supreme simplicity in your holiday wardrobe is as freeing as leaving your BlackBerry at home. Incessant communication wasn't an issue in 1944, when Humphrey Bogart and Lauren Bacall sailed away in their plain-as-can-be yet sublime cottons, but the iconic Hollywood sweethearts are still an inspiring vision of perfection.

THERE AND BACK

It is possible to look stylish while in transit without subscribing to the Elizabeth Taylor school of travel, circa 1967, which requires a two-piece suit, matching hat, high heels and thirty-two pieces of Louis Vuitton luggage. And it's important: It may be just an airport, but you never know whom you'll run into. Besides, your appearance sets the tone for the rest of your trip. Comfort is key, but it should never look as though it is your main criteria. What you need: body-skimming styles in breathable fabrics, a snuggly but not cumbersome knit in merino with some stretch to keep its shape, a killer jacket or coat that you can whisk on at the end, sunglasses and some shoes that will accommodate swollen feet. They don't have to be flat, just humane. Keep the grooming simple, but keep it. What else you'll need: a chic ponytail, a face spritz, decanted containers of essential beauty faves and hand cream.

GET PACKING

How you transport your possessions is as crucial as what you transport. These days everyone needs wheels. Ideally, a case should be sturdy to protect against breakage but not too heavy. Redistributing your belongings in front of fifty irate people because you're over the weight limit is an unamusing start to your trip. Keep the carry-on light. Everything beyond a book, an iPod, the aforementioned beauty items, some wet wipes, a cashmere shawl and cashmere socks is superfluous. But coddle yourself. This is your mini world for now.

Learn to love packing. The process can be highly instructive, spotlighting the everyday and magnifying it until you either realize you can't live without a particular item or wonder what possessed you to bring it along. Assuming you packed the things you love best, what are they? And what do they tell you about your style?

Brigitte
Bardot

HOW TO PACK LIKE A PRO

• CHOOSE YOUR WEAPONS WISELY

Suitcase technology has come quite far.
If your luggage is anywhere near its decade
anniversary, consider updating. The best
options are lightweight with strong but
flexible exteriors and rugged wheels. Also
on the requirement checklist: a deceptively
deep interior with lots of side pockets.

• BE AN EARLY BIRD

Set out your suitcase a few days before
your departure and start to fill it with what
you think you might need. Once you're
ready to finalize, edit your selections down
to a perfect capsule. Nothing causes over-
packing like a harried race to the finish.

• DIVIDE AND CONQUER

To maintain eternal tidiness, the secret is
using bags within bags. Dispense with
plastic sacks in favor of inexpensive see-
through or mesh pouches to separate
clothes and accessories into easy-to-access
portions. This will expedite everything
from random airport searches to quickly
locating your favorite bikini.

• EMBRACE INDIVIDUALITY

There's no room for copycats in the smart
suitcase. Stay on the lookout for wardrobe
redundancies, particularly when it comes
to bulky pieces like knits, sweatshirts
and footwear. Be creative in making pieces
multitask and earn their place on the trip.

"Personal style is knowing yourself, your lifestyle, your body and finding clothes that become the frame. You become the star. It's knowing when to say yes and when to say no."

—MICHAEL KORS

For some women, holidays are like a release clause: a chance to play at being bangle-happy hippies when back home they're sleek, executive warriors. For others, a holiday wardrobe can be an illuminating microcosm of their everyday closet. Whichever scenario is true for you, the same rules apply. Choose a color scheme of three or four hues that sing in harmony. Focus on one vibe. (Alternating flamenco, grunge and Forties retro may work for you at home, but no suitcase is large enough to facilitate all those looks on tour.) Finally, identify your star turns. It could be a dress, a jacket or an amazing skirt. It doesn't matter, provided everything works with everything else.

You probably don't need more than two star pieces for a week's trip. Or three if you're planning on some night action. Make the fourth a coat that can be styled up or down and wear it en route. Now, before you pack, lay everything out around your stars until you have a self-sufficient constellation: a handful of tops, accessories (two colorful scarves, one small evening clutch) and three or four pairs of shoes. A decade ago packing experts advised two pairs, one for day, the other for night. That's before shoes became a fast track to transforming your look.

CONQUERING THE COLD, BEATING THE HEAT

Once you're in the habit of thinking in capsule form, you'll find it holds for any trip. For skiing, two ski jackets, one pair of dark ski pants and one top for every day you're away is plenty. Even with a packed après-ski schedule, you'll need fewer items than you think, which is fortunate because these clothes tend to be bulky. A couple pairs of velvet jeans, some thin sweaters—as most ski accommodation is overheated—a fabulous vest and you're done.

It doesn't take more than five bikinis to make a holiday, especially if you wear them in rotation and mix and match. You're bound to buy at least one more while there. In fact bikinis, sarongs and sandals are items you can buy guilt free on holiday on the grounds that they're evergreen classics and that the best ones are found far from home. Do your homework so that when you get to Morocco or India, you know what's worth buying (the jewels, the embroidered shawls—some of which will even work once you're immersed back in real life). Nota bene: Walk away from the $700 caftan or the $500 bikini. It's the equivalent to a romantic fling—exciting at the time but with short-lived appeal. Once you get it home it's going to spend the rest of the year packed away, waiting for the next trip.

But bikinis aren't really the issue. Unlike your beloved Hermès Birkin, they don't hog space. Yes, you love that bag, but was it really the right choice for the beach? Sometimes love does mean having to say sorry—to your favorite possession—see you in a fortnight. Round out the swimwear with a lot of white and some loose linen pants, a clutch of caftans, a beautiful sarong (indulge your love of extroverted patterns, which always look better in the sun), a few tanks and T-shirts and inexpensive gold and silver jewelry, which looks better and better as you tan. In place of that Birkin, grab a chic canvas tote that looks as good on the plane as it does on the beach.

AND EVERYTHING IN BETWEEN

How to enjoy a typical chilly summer's day in Scotland or San Francisco and other four-climates-in-one-day destinations? Pull together a mixture of silk, cashmere and merino-wool layers that can be stacked up or stripped off as the temperature dips and soars. A good base is the cotton jersey T-shirt dress that goes as well with a chunky cardigan as it does slipped over a silk camisole. And always bring some closed-toe shoes, preferably ones you can wear with cashmere socks. It's amazingly hard to feel stylish with cold feet.

Demi
Moore in
*Charlie's
Angels*

SWIMWEAR 101

• ONE OR TWO?

Your first question: bikini or one-piece
suit? Take stock of your midsection.
It doesn't need to be washboard flat, but
if you're dealing with saggy skin or
a bit of a pouch, a sleek one-piece is your
best option. On the other hand, if you're
not rail thin but have hourglass curves, a
bikini is ideal to highlight your assets.

• SHAPE BY DESIGN

Use stylish swimsuit details to gently
disguise and divert attention from figure
flaws. A chic asymmetrical neckline,
for instance, can give a tummy-obscuring
one-piece new energy. Retro-inspired
ruching and plunged necklines also cover
all manner of sins.

• SIZE MATTERS

Don't be tempted to buy a suit a bit
small in hopes of dieting your way into
it or simply because wearing a size
up is distressing. A great bathing suit is
all about fit, numbers be damned.

• SHOP OPTIMALLY

The ideal conditions to find swim perfection: a healthy chunk of time in an
uncrowded store with both a wide
selection and a knowledgeable staff. Look
for a specialty swimwear boutique or a
lingerie shop that also sells bathing suits.
And try to get a bikini wax beforehand.

COOL IN THE HEAT

• RHAPSODIZE BOHEMIAN

Even if your style isn't remotely flower child–esque, take your general cues from this free-spirited look. Think about loose, simple clothes in light and natural fabrics that don't feel like work to wear. Trade stilettos for flat sandals, but if you simply can't live without a little lift, opt for an espadrille wedge.

• LEAVE TRENDS BEHIND

There's a wonderful timeless quality to vacation ensembles. Jacqueline Onassis's white jeans and oversized shades would be right at home in current-day Capri. But that means those extreme and of-the-moment pieces in your wardrobe are out of place on a sandy shore. Don't worry. They'll still be there waiting for you when you return.

• SEEK ESSENTIAL PERFECTION

Spend a little time to find trans–cendent versions of the few important building blocks of your holiday kit, which includes sunglasses, a straw bag, a hat, a bathing suit and a cover-up.

Audrey Hepburn

Chloë Sevigny

Dasha
Zhukova

Kate
Moss

Jacqueline
Onassis

With clothing at a minimum, beachy extras like a straw bag, colorful cuff or tooled leather sandals, have their moment in the sun.

HOT IN THE COLD

• A TOUCH OF LUXE

The bad news: Staying stylish in subzero mountain climes is often dependent on high-end wares crafted from thick, multi-ply cashmere, fur and shearling. There is good news, however. It takes only one fabulous piece paired with jeans or leggings and sturdy boots to craft a look with impact.

• FAUX? SURE

Fake fur has improved by leaps and bounds in just the past decade. Faux vests, jackets and coats not only look good, they are also less expensive and can be quite warm (though not quite as warm as the real thing). Be sure to compensate with an extra layer before heading outside or hitting the slopes.

• WHITE NIGHTS (AND DAYS)

Incorporating shades of white—ivory, cream, eggshell, et cetera—into your winter holiday wardrobe is a refreshing way to lighten up dark and heavy-looking ensembles.

Bianca
Brandolini d'Adda

Jessica
Alba

Finish snowbound looks with a
sleek pair of aviators and a
utilitarian leather satchel.

AIRPORT STYLE

• COMFORT WITH CARE

Women don't dress for flights
like they used to. Still, there's a
happy medium between sweats
and a skirt suit. The look can
be as easy as slim jeans with a
smart cardigan, big scarf and
ballet flats—or a variation on
that theme. You can trade flats
for boots and jeans for leggings,
either in leather or thick cotton.

• TAKE A LOAD OFF

Particularly for long hauls,
there's a temptation to take
it all with you—magazines,
books, laptop, iPod, snacks
and more. But there's nothing
stylish about dragging an
overstuffed and weighty bag
through a busy transit hub.
Keep your carry-on—whether a
tote or a weekender—to a man-
ageable size and be strict about
streamlining its contents.

• DON'T JUMP THE GUN

You might be headed to
Hawaii, but you're leaving from
Detroit. So dress appropriately
for the climate of your origin,
and then lose some layers when
you arrive.

Reese
Witherspoon

Rihanna

170

Miranda
Kerr

Cheryl
Cole

Eva
Mendes

Traveling in style
means traveling light
with a chunky sweater,
comfortable but chic
flats, a luxe weekender
and not much more.

171

CHAPTER 9

THE BEAUTY FACTOR

Creating a signature look goes beyond a perfect wardrobe. Enter the cosmetics counter and salon.

FACE VALUE

The role of beauty—whether bright crimson lips or a gorgeous mane of curls—in creating a signature look is invaluable but occasionally overlooked. Nevertheless, hair and makeup and even perfume are intrinsic to great style.

MANY WOMEN UNDERESTIMATE JUST HOW POWerful a tool makeup can be when it comes to personal style. Yet it's also impossible to imagine Madonna's succession of transformative guises, Linda Evangelista's unforgettable presence in some of the most memorable fashion images of the nineties or Joan Crawford's emphatic, enduring features without input from the cosmetics counter and salon.

THE SHORT CUT WITH A LONG LIFE

"I've been to Vidal Sassoon," announced Mia Farrow in a famed celluloid beauty moment in the 1968 film *Rosemary's Baby*. The legendary hairstylist actually had cut her hair for the film, but Farrow had taken to the pixie crop a couple years earlier. Still, the new 'do was like hitting the refresh button—as it still is—exposing the young actress's exquisite bone structure and imparting a lovely waifish innocence. It's no surprise that Farrow's haircut is still the go-to reference for short hair over four decades later.

Paris March 2100

MAKING YOUR MARK

A strong beauty signature needn't be brash. Rachel Weisz's dark, prominent eyebrows, Cate Blanchett's smoky kohl, Kate Bosworth's peachy glow and Kate Winslet's coral lips are subtle manifestations of the art of the brush. The important first step is to assess your features. Can they take a slash of scarlet and a monochromatic complexion like Paloma Picasso, or

 Personal style is dressing who you are, not what the trends dictate. Style should capture the soul: the romantic, the eccentric, the expressive. Dress with integrity and conviction. They are the only two labels you need.

—JOHN GALLIANO,
CREATIVE DIRECTOR,
CHRISTIAN DIOR

are they better suited to the softer blending, highlighting and shading that a fine-featured beauty like Natalie Portman deploys? Be bold. Sometimes a prominent feature isn't the one that needs camouflaging but accentuating. Cindy Crawford's mole was what gave her perfectly pretty face character. Barbra Streisand would not be who she is without that magnificent nose. Even if you decide your makeup look is a no-makeup look, à la Tilda Swinton, Stella Tennant or Reese Witherspoon, you need to protect and prime your skin if you're to look polished.

TRENDS IN A BOTTLE

Makeup is one of the easiest ways to access a fashion trend that doesn't depend on weight, height or bank account. Never going back to the full-skirted prom look? You can still channel the fifties and early sixties with a flick of Audrey Hepburn–esque black eyeliner. Not quite prepared to splurge on Chanel's jade-green tweed jacket? Then grab the coordinating nail polish instead. In fact, funky-colored nails are probably the single fastest (and most fun) route to displaying your fashion credentials.

Conversely, few things carbon-date a woman as brutally as her undying allegiance to the beauty trends of her youth. As skin matures and contours alter, so do cosmetic needs. It doesn't mean that you have to abandon what you love. Maybe Jean Shrimpton's sooty eyes no longer work, but you could achieve the same definition using modern eye pencils to create a dark, soft streak of chocolate or navy blue on your upper lid. Be honest with yourself, and if you can't see things objectively, ask a good friend if that Brigitte Bardot–esque updo is still working for you.

THOSE WHO TEACH

Just as today's pigments and textures have immeasurably improved, so have those advisors behind the beauty counters. Many can execute—and show you how to create—a sophisticated look, be it barely there or Theda Bara–worthy vamp. Do your homework (Bobbi Brown's the queen of natural, Dior's more overt) and take advantage of their expertise. Get the advisors at the Laura Mercier counter to apply your individual lashes for you. (For the price of a single purchase, they'll do it gratis.) Or you can always ask the sales consultant whose handiwork you most admire to create a party look on your way to the fete from the office.

THE POWER OF SCENT

OUT OF SIGHT BUT NOT MIND • Since scent doesn't have visual impact, it's generally not the first topic that comes up when discussing personal style. However, fragrance can be an integral element when you're considering how you present yourself to the world. If you find "the one," it can be a compelling statement about your individuality.

ENTER THE PERFUME-IVERSE • And what a big place it is to explore. Acquaint yourself with the six major types. Floral: flowery and feminine. Citrus: crisp, lightly fruity and clean. Oriental: warm, musky and spicy. Chypre: woodsy and rich yet fresh. Fougère: outdoorsy and light, often described as green. Gourmand: sweet and food inspired, like vanilla.

THEN THE BEAUTY COUNTER • Shopping for perfume shouldn't be rushed. Identifying one or two types you like will help narrow your search. Try a couple while shopping but take home as many samples as you can to test-drive at your leisure to find what really works for you. Keep in mind, the notes of a scent—top, middle, and base—emerge over time.

DAB, SPRITZ, DAZZLE • Wearing your favorite scent is delicate work. It should be noticeable but not distracting. Spray or dab the pulse points— your throat and wrists. (Don't rub wrists together; the friction can distort the scent.) Then choose another spot like the nape of the neck or crook of your arm. Experiment until you find the perfect amount.

EAU MY!

Though invisible, scent is a personal, evocative and invaluable style stamp. Never settle for imitations or mass herd pleasers. When choosing, start with the classics. They've lasted for a reason. Don't be afraid to explore bespoke options, of which there are many today. Frederic Malle, Francis Kurkdjian and Le Labo are all pleasurable starting points. You'll know you've got it right when you can't stop sniffing yourself. As for how much to use, never spray it on so thickly you leave an echo chamber in your wake. Leave them wanting more.

TRESSED OUT

Finally, there's the exclamation mark that is hair. Few so-called trivial subjects provoke as much outrage or comments. Debbie Harry built an initial career (and persona) on a sexy jagged blonde bob. Roman Polanski paid Vidal Sassoon the then extravagant sum of $5,000 to fly from London to Los Angeles to finesse Mia Farrow's elfin crop for *Rosemary's Baby* in 1967. Jackie Kennedy skillfully toed the line between stately and youthful with her tousled beehive (and provided a sexy counterpoint to her first lady uniform). Want to make a silent declaration about a life-changing event? Change your locks. Go blonde (Nicole Kidman), slice it off (Katie Holmes) or let it grow (Halle Berry). Or simply announce to the world that you're still here, still sexy (Diane Sawyer).

For some fortunate women, a single hairdo seemingly becomes a life long affirmation of their character: the glamorous and sporty Louise Brooks bob, Sofia Coppola's low-maintenance shoulder-length version or Goldie Hawn's bubbly, ageless cascade. But look closely and they're constantly updating by adding highlights or subtracting a few layers.

BROW UNIVERSITY

• GO PRO

Your eyebrows have the important job of framing your face. Unless yours are naturally perfect, seek the skills of a professional to craft a flattering shape. Don't trust them to just anyone. Get recommendations from trusted sources. Recovering from a mishap isn't easy.

• NATURAL SELECTION

Your goal is to look polished, but your brow guru's work shouldn't advertise itself. Anything that's too sharply defined or too widely spaced isn't ideal. Err on the side of slightly undone instead of excessively manicured.

• THE SHAPE OF THINGS

For the most part, your bone structure serves as a general guide. But there is room to subtly tweak to favorable effect within that framework. An angled arch, for instance, can slim a round face, while a graceful curve complements a long face.

• TOP-NOTCH TOOLS

The time between your visits to an aesthetician will vary widely, but brows require touches of maintenance at least once a week. Your basic needs: a pair of high-quality tweezers, a brow brush and a clear gel for hold.

THE BASICS OF HAIR

A CUT ABOVE • A great haircut is a lot like a beautiful, well-designed dress. Both use someone else's talent and skill to make your life more effortlessly stylish. An adroit stylist should be able to give you a solid framework that plays up your hair's particular strengths so that your 'do looks polished and pretty with minimal effort.

L USH LOCKS • Between chemical dyes and the heat of styling tools, your hair's health can suffer. Pay attention to any changes in weight or texture to monitor any damage. Reconsider your regimen if you see anything drastic. Give your tresses the occasional vacation with an air-dry and regularly use a deep conditioner. Healthy hair is stylish hair.

E VOLUTION OR REVOLUTION • Classic looks have their virtues, but a hairstyle that's a decade or so old can make you look past your prime, even if your clothes are à la mode. The change doesn't need to be drastic. Shifting the length or adding layers should be sufficient. On the other hand, a brand new 'do can renew energy.

N IGHT AND DAY • Hair is an important part of an evening look. A lovely little updo or sleek chignon opens up the neckline of a cocktail dress or gown with considerable charm. But formal styles are frequently too shellacked or frothy. Stay light on the hairspray and inject a little daytime ease into the nighttime look.

Leighton
Meester

Thandie
Newton

Jennifer
Connelly

Carey
Mulligan

MAKEUP ESSENTIALS

SKIN DEEP • Great style starts with a clear and smooth face. Avoid blemishes by cleaning your skin properly and investing in a facial at least twice a year. Use a light concealer or foundation and dusting of powder to cover dark spots and balance tone. For evening, try a product with a hint of shimmer as a highlighter.

THE EYES HAVE IT • For day, use a coat of mascara and a sweep of neutral-hued shadow to subtly define and darken. For evening, you can refresh your day look and focus on bright lips, or make your eyes the focus with a deeper color of shadow and eyeliner.

LIP SERVICE • For daytime, a beautiful matte lipstick might be the only makeup you wear. Choose something with rich color that's not too bright. For evening, choose between lips and eyes. Pair heavily made-up eyes with a pale lip gloss, or go light on the eyeshadow and make a statement with an intense pink or red lip.

CHEEK TO CHEEK • Blush should never be obvious. Your goal is a natural-looking flush. (One exception is *Harper's Bazaar* legend Diana Vreeland who wore heavy rouge out to her ears.) Whether you're using a powder or a light cream, apply a small amount to the tops of your cheekbones and blend from there. Add as needed.

Rachel
McAdams

Kate
Bosworth

Kerry
Washington

Emma
Watson

CHAPTER 10

BUILDING
A FOUNDATION

First things last. Being stylish
requires the correct pieces
to wear under your clothes.

THE FIRST BRICK

As counterintuitive as it is to spend good time and money on a part of your wardrobe that isn't often seen, assembling a smart collection of underpinnings is a step that shouldn't be skipped or skimped on.

FROM BURNING BRAS TO METAL CONICAL CUPS THAT launch fireworks (thank Lady Gaga for that), underwear has maintained a pivotal cultural and countercultural position in social history for the past forty years. What you're wearing under your clothes even has the power to change your mood. No wonder the female cast of *Mad Men* wears authentic 1960s pieces. Lingerie can make us feel sexier, sleeker or sportier. It can emphasize youth (Scarlett Johansson's pale cotton briefs in *Lost in Translation*) or womanliness (Mrs. Robinson's black lace brassiere). On a pragmatic note, it can subtly change our posture and transform the way a dress hangs.

NIGHTS IN WHITE SATIN

Since the sixties, the full slip has slipped out of the collective consciousness as a wardrobe necessity. But to see Elizabeth Taylor, both in 1960's *Butterfield 8* (pictured here) and *Cat on a Hot Tin Roof* a couple years earlier, is reason enough to reconsider the lace-and-satin creation as an unmentionable that might have a place in your closet, to wear under a dress or simply lounge in at home.

FORM A SUPPORT GROUP

A proper lingerie wardrobe must meet every neckline requirement and solve all the issues that crop up when you opt for a pair of extra-low-rise pants or a very clingy fabric. While the workings may be invisible, the end results are anything but. You wouldn't build a house without a foundation. Why scrimp on your own underpinnings? This isn't about quantity or extravagance but about spending what it takes. If you're fortunate enough

 Personal style is what drives you to be an individual, whether it be clothing, music, art, jewelry, opinion, et cetera. [It is] being who you are and being proud of where you are from. I injected this message into a recent collection that was very multicultural. I took a sprig of this and a dash of that and before you knew it, I touched upon so many cultures that define me, I felt as if I had walked around the world. "

—JEAN-PAUL GAULTIER

to find the perfect fit in Calvin Klein or Victoria's Secret, then you really won't have to spend a fortune. For thongs and briefs, it's even less of a hurdle. But if you end up having to shop for bras from pricier labels, bite the bullet and just buy fewer.

An all-purpose bra wardrobe should include a multistrap version for halternecks and strapless and asymmetrical dresses. Invest in one with straps that aren't too difficult to adjust or remove. Seamless T-shirt bras, usually padded to a greater or lesser degree, are the workhorses of lingerie. Nude shades go under anything, so ensure you have at least two or three. You'll need at least one black one for wearing under dark clothes, and add a jewel tone or bright color for fun. Lace bras remain the mark of a femme fatale, but they've had to get with the modern multitasking woman's program. As a result, many are now nonscratchy and fine enough to work under the clingiest fabrics.

If you've never been properly fitted, don't be surprised if you find yourself weeping with relief the first time you wear a bra that does just that.

A staggering number of women still buy the wrong size, all of which could be avoided if we took a little time to seek help from professional fitters who really know their stuff. If you've never been properly fitted, don't be surprised if you find yourself weeping with relief the first time you wear a bra that does just that.

AND A TOUCH OF LACE

One ravishingly pretty camisole from Sabbia Rosa or La Perla might seem an extravagance. (It's amazing how much a tiny quantity of lace and silk can cost.) But this is one piece of underwear we can all wear as outerwear, slipped under masculine jackets or dresses with deep armholes. It's a classic, gorgeous problem solver you'll wear over and over again. Add a flesh-toned power-mesh slip to wear under slinky dresses and avoid static. It's the twenty-first-century's answer to the corset.

HOW TO BUY THE RIGHT BRA

DO YOUR HOMEWORK • You may very well have become accustomed to an ill-fitting bra—one that digs into your shoulders, causes bulging or requires constant adjusting. The first step is to simply pay attention and make note of any chronic issues with the bras you already own.

THE MEASURED APPROACH • Your exact size might surprise you. Measure directly under your bust and straight across your rib cage, then add five to determine band size. Do this again across the fullest part of your bust. Calculate cup size by subtracting the first measurement from the second. The difference corresponds to the letter, i.e., two inches equals a B cup.

ASK AN EXPERT • Since fitting services are often free, there's no excuse not to use a professional (although there is the expectation that you'll be making a purchase). She'll also be able to recommend solutions for specific pieces of clothing. Get fitted (or measure yourself) regularly since bust size shifts with weight changes.

THE PRICE OF RIGHT • It may pain you to spend your clothing budget on pieces that aren't visible, but a good bra is worth a few more dollars. It can improve both your posture and the line of your clothes. And if washed with care, air-dried and not worn every day, a high-quality specimen can last longer than a year.

LINGERIE ESSENTIALS

BRA NECESSITIES • You should have a collection of bras that covers most situations. Along with six or seven everyday basics in nude and black, make sure to have a strapless bra, one with convertible straps, one that's lined for clingy tops, a demi cup for low necklines and a sturdy sports bra.

BOTTOM LINE • A visible panty line (a.k.a. VPL) is never acceptable. Luckily, wearing either a soft cotton thong or microfiber boy short with tight clothing is an easy solution. The same goes for underwear that's visible above low-riding pants, which should be worn with equally low-cut briefs. Also be sure to regularly discard underwear that's past its prime.

THE ENABLERS • Sheer blouses and tight dresses beg the question of how to wear them. The answer: with slips, camisoles, opaque tights and shapewear. A couple of camisoles and full slips in nude and black fill most fashion needs. Shapewear like Spanx can smooth and hold any area—tummy, thighs—you deem a problem.

LOUNGE ACT • You don't need to kick back at home in lace and satin, but do trade your old shredded high school T-shirt for new soft cotton tanks and pants in pretty pale shades (or a similar self-respecting alternative). Also a necessity: a good robe, whether it's terry cloth, light knit or even silk.

THE UNDER STATEMENT

• A LOOK WITH LEGS

Even simple black opaque or sheer hosiery has an impact on your ensemble. But also consider lace tights, Swiss-dot sheers or jewel-tone opaques to update your black dress. Just be careful with splashy patterns, which work on only the young and coltish.

• LET IT SHOW

Some lingerie details are too pretty to keep to yourself. Unmentionables that should occasionally be allowed to peek out into the light of day: lace-trimmed camisoles, Victorian-inspired petticoats, the strap of a brightly hued bra and a bustier or corset.

• TOP BRAS

Is it a top or is it a bra? This hybrid item is one of those great multitasking pieces. It should, of course, be more top than bra if more than just the strap is visible, i.e., not sheer. But worn with a cardigan and pencil skirt, the bra top creates a fashion-forward look with subtle sex appeal.

Zoë
Saldana

Alexa
Chung

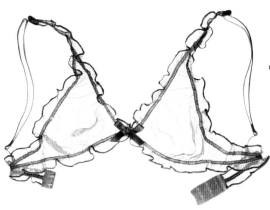

Show off a glimpse of a beautiful piece of lingerie, like a lace-trimmed camisole or a ruffled bra.

Index

Photography and Illustration Credits

Page opposite Title Page Illustration by Karl Lagerfeld.

Pages following Title Page Illustration by Donna Karan. Illustration by Dolce & Gabbana.

CHAPTER 1
WHAT IS PERSONAL STYLE?
Page 8 Terry Tsiolis. Model: Toni Garrn. **Page 11** Tropical Press Agency/Getty Images. **Page 13** Keystone/Getty Images. **Page 14** Illustration by Frida Giannini. **Page 19** Christian Deville/Apis/Sygma/Corbis. **Pages 20—21**, clockwise from top left: Sunset Boulevard/Corbis; Hulton Archive/Getty Images; George Hurrell/John Kobal Foundation/Getty Images; Scotty Welbourne/John Kobal Foundation/Getty Images; John Kobal Collection/Getty Images; FPG/Hulton Archive/Getty Images; Hulton Archive/Getty Images. **Pages 22—23**, clockwise from top left: Peter Stackpole/Time Life Pictures/Getty Images; Arnold Newman/Getty Images; AP Photo; Bettmann/Corbis; Transcendental Graphics/Getty Images. **Pages 24—25**, clockwise from top left: Paul Guglielmo/Apis/Sygma/Corbis; Omnia/Globe Photos Inc.; Dove/Express/Getty Images; Jim Gray/Keystone/Hulton Archive/Getty Images. **Pages 26—27**, clockwise from top right: Ron Galella/WireImage; Rose Hartman/Getty Images; David Levenson/Getty Images; Ron Galella/WireImage; Michael Ohs Archives/Getty Images; Terry O'Neill/Getty Images. **Pages 28—29**, clockwise from top left: Gene Shaw/Time Life Pictures/Getty Images; Lawrence Schwartzwald/Sygma/Corbis; Paul Hawthorne/Getty Images; Hector Vallenilla/pacificcoastnews.com; Jim Young/Reuters/Corbis; Jim Smeal/WireImage. **Page 31**: James Devaney/WireImage.

CHAPTER 2
HOW TO FIND YOUR LOOK
Page 32 Terry Tsiolis. Model: Toni Garrn. **Page 35** Eric Ryan/Getty Images. **Page 38** Illustration by Alber Elbaz. **Page 43** Illustration by Vera Wang. **Pages 44—45**, clockwise from top left: Christopher Peterson/BuzzPhoto/FilmMagic; Fred Duval/FilmMagic; Dimitrios Kambouris/WireImage; Kevin Mazur/WireImage; Chance Yeh/patrickmcmullan.com; Steven A Henry/Getty Images; Stefania D'Alessandro/WireImage; Eric Feferberg/AFP/Getty Images. **Pages 46—47**, clockwise from top left: Jon Kopaloff/FilmMagic; Eugene Gologursky/WireImage; Dave M. Benett/Getty Images; Gerald Herbert/AP Photo; Chance Yeh/patrickmcmullan.com; Pascal Le Segretain/Getty Images; Frazer Harrison/Getty Images; Venturelli/WireImage. **Pages 48—49**, from left: Evan Agostini/Getty Images; Mirek Towski/DMI/Time Life Pictures/Getty Images; Gregg DeGuire/WireImage (2);; Chris Jackson/Getty Images; Michael Buckner/WireImage. **Pages 50—51**, from left: Mel Bouzad/Rex USA/BEImages; Nikos Vinieratos/Rex USA/BEImages; Dennis Stone/Rex USA/BEImages; Rex USA/BEImages; Matt Baron/BEImages; Larry Busacca/Getty Images. **Pages 52—53**, from left: Ron Galella/WireImage; Jim Smeal/WireImage; Vince Bucci/Getty Images; J.Vespa/WireImage; Eric Ryan/Getty Images; Michael Tran/FimMagic. **Pages 54—55**, rom left: Brad Barket/Getty Images; Yuji Ohsugi/WireImage; Frank Micelotta/Getty Images; Everett Collection/Rex USA/BEImages; Eric

Ryan/Getty Images; Jeffrey Mayer/WireImage.

Pages 56—57, clockwise from top left: Gilbert Carrasquillo/FilmMagic; Kevin Mazur/WireImage; Ron Sachs-Pool/Getty Images; Chip Somodevilla/Getty Images (2); Brooks Kraft/Corbis; Dave M. Benett/Getty Images; Fred Duval/FilmMagic. **Pages 58—59**, clockwise from top left: Brian Ach/WireImage; Larry Busacca/Getty Images; Eric Ryan/Getty Images; Dave M. Benett/Getty Images; Lydie/SIPA; Gustavo Caballero/Getty Images; Joe Schildhorn/patrickmcmullan.com; Billy Farrell/patrickmcmullan.com.

Pages 60—61, clockwise from top left: Steve Granitz/WireImage; Fotonoticias/WireImage; Matt Baron/BEImages; James Devaney/WireImage; Frazer Harrison/Getty Images; Fotonoticias/WireImage; Gustavo Caballero/Getty Images; Frazer Harrison/Getty Images. **Pages 62—63**, clockwise from top left: Denise Truscello/WireImage; Ray Tamarra/Getty Images; Larry Busacca/Getty Images; John Shearer/WireImage; Amy Sussman/Getty Images; Donato Sardella/WireImage; Dave M. Benett/Getty Images; Joe Kohen/WireImage.

**CHAPTER 3
THE ART
OF SHOPPING**

Page 64 Terry Richardson. Model: Magdalena Frackowiak. **Page 67** Courtesy Everett Collection. **Page 68** Illustration by Diane von Furstenberg. **Page 76**, clockwise from top left: Courtesy Cartier; courtesy Verdura; Davies + Starr (2); Jesus Ayala/Studio D. **Pages 78—79**, clockwise from top left: Charlotte Jenks Lewis/Studio D; Jean Baptiste Lacroix/FilmMagic; Eric Ryan/Getty Images; Dominique Charriau/WireImage; Jesus Ayala/Studio D; Billy Farrell/patrickmcmullan.com (2).

**CHAPTER 4
A WARDROBE THAT
WORKS**

Page 83 Camilla Akrans. Model: Kendra Spears. **Page 85** Burt Glinn/Magnum Photos. **Page 87** Illustration by Francisco Costa. **Page 88** Illustration by Ralph Lauren. **Pages 92—93**, clockwise from top left: Davies + Starr; Andrew H. Walker/Getty Images; Henry Lamb/Photowire/BEImages; Dominique Charriau/WireImage; Todd Huffman; Courtesy Eddie Borgo; Dan & Corina

Lecca (2). **Pages 94—95**, clockwise from top left: Davies + Starr; Dan & Corina Lecca (3); Davies + Starr; Richard Majchrzak/Studio D; Dan & Corina Lecca (2).**Pages 96—97**, clockwise from top left: Davies + Starr; Matt Baron/BEImages; David Livingston/Getty Images; Joe Kohen/WireImage; Charlotte Jenks Lewis/Studio D; courtesy Paige Novick; Gilbert Carrasquillo/FilmMagic; Dave M. Benett/Getty Images.

**CHAPTER 5
OFF-DUTY CHIC**

Page 98—99 Greg Kadel. Model: Regina Feoktistova. **Page 101** John Springer Collection/Corbis. **Page 104** Illustration by Phillip Jones for Stella McCartney. **Pages 108—109**, clockwise from top left: Kevin Sweeney/Studio D; Almasi/Torres/bauergriffinonline.com; Dominique Charriau/WireImage; Splash News; Davies + Starr; Todd Huffman; Dan & Corina Lecca (2). **Pages 110—111**, clockwise from top left: Davies + Starr; Dan & Corina Lecca (3); courtesy Tod's; Charlotte Jenks Lewis/Studio D; Dan & Corina Lecca (2). **Pages 112—113**, clockwise from top left: Charlotte Lewis

Jenks/Studio D; Dan & Corina Lecca (3); Marko Metzinger/Studio D; Nils Friedman/Studio D; Dan & Corina Lecca (2). **Pages 114—115**, clockwise from top left: Charlotte Jenks Lewis/Studio D; Rex USA/BEImages; Dominique Charriau/ WireImage; Snapper Media/Splash News; Richard Majchrzak/Studio D; Davies + Starr; Richard Young/Rex Features/ Rex USA/BEImages; David Aguilera/BuzzFoto/ FilmMagic. **Pages 116— 117**, clockwise from top left: Richard Majchrzak/ Studio D; Billy Farrell/ patrickmcmullan.com; London Entertainment/ Splash News; Kevin Mazur/WireImage; Charlotte Jenks Lewis/ Studio D; courtesy Hayden-Harnett; Dan & Corina Lecca (2).

CHAPTER 6
EVENING GLAMOUR
Page 118 Greg Kadel. Model: Maryna Linchuk. **Page 121** Alfred Eisenstaedt/Time Life Pictures/Getty Images. **Page 122** Illustration by Giorgio Armani.**Page 125** Bettman/Corbis. **Pages 128—129**, clockwise from top left: Davies + Starr; Kevin Mazur/WireImage; Malcolm Taylor/Getty Images; Kevin Kane/Getty Images; courtesy Carelle; Davies + Starr; Rabbani & Solimene/WireImage; Stephen Lovekin/Getty Images. **Pages 130—131**, clockwise from top left: Davies + Starr; Billy Farrell/patrickmcmullan. com; Mike Coppola/ FilmMagic; Mark Von Holden/WireImage; Jesus Ayala/Studio D; Kevin Mazur/WireImage; Nick Harvey/WireImage. **Pages 132—133**, clockwise from top left: Davies + Starr; Ferdaus Shamim/WireImage; Jim Spellman/WireImage; Daniele Venturelli/ WireImage; courtesy Daniel Swarovski;; Dan & Corina Lecca (2). **Pages 134—135**, clockwise from top left: Davies + Starr; Foc Kan/WireImage; Matt Baron/BEImages; Patrick McMullan/ patrickmcmullan.com; Davies + Starr; courtesy Mish New York; Dan & Corina Lecca (2). **Pages 136—137**, clockwise from top left: Alberto E. Rodriguez/Getty Images; Davies + Starr; courtesy Givenchy; Darryl Patterson; courtesy Bulgari; Davies + Starr; Frazer Harrison/ Getty Images.

CHAPTER 7
ESSENTIAL EXTRAS
Page 138 Greg Kadel. Model: Maryna Linchuk.

Page 141 Express/ Getty Images. **Page 143**, clockwise from top left: Kevin Sweeney/Studio D; Davies + Starr; Richard Majchrzak/Studio D; Kevin Sweeney/Studio D (2). **Page 144** Illustration by Bruno Frisoni. **Pages 148—149**, clockwise from left: Ian Gavan/Getty Images; John Shearer/ WireImage; Davies + Starr (4); Todd Huffman; Davies + Starr. **Pages 150—151**, clockwise from left: Christopher Peterson/BuzzFoto/ FilmMagic; Mike Marsland/ WireImage; Davies + Starr (2); courtesy Brian Atwood; Kevin Sweeney/Studio D; courtesy Charlotte Olympia. **Pages 152—153**, clockwise from left: Julien Hekimian/WireImage; Jason LaVeris/FilmMagic; Davies + Starr; courtesy Bottega Veneta; Richard Majchrzak/Studio D; Jesus Ayala/Studio D; Davies + Starr. **Pages 154—155**, clockwise from top left: Davies + Starr; Amber de Vos/patrickmcmullan. com; Zach Hyman/ patrickmcmullan.com; Stefania D'Alessandro/ Getty Images; Jesus Ayala/ Studio D; Kevin Sweeney/ Studio D; Splash News; Ron Asadorian/Splash News.

CHAPTER 8
THE GETAWAY

Page 156 Tom Munro. Model: Sigrid Agren. **Page 159** Archive Photos/Getty Images. **Page 161** Araldo Crollalanza/Rex USA/BEImages. **Page 162** Illustration by Michael Kors. **Page 165** Columbia/courtesy Everett Collection. **Pages 166—167**, clockwise from top left: Charlotte Jenks Lewis/Studio D; Splash News; KCSPresse/Splash News; Lino Nanni/Globe Photos; Charlotte Jenks Lewis/Studio D; Davies + Starr; Brian Prahl/Splash News; Rex Features/courtesy Everett Collection. **Pages 168—169**, clockwise from top left: Davies + Starr; Dan & Corina Lecca (3); Davies + Starr; Ray Tamara/Getty Images; Marco Balsarini/Zuma Press. **Pages 170—171**, clockwise from top left: Charlotte Jenks Lewis/Studio D; GVK/bauergriffinonline.com; TS/Splash News; Matingas/bauergriffinonline.com; Davies + Starr; Charlotte Jenks Lewis/Studio D; Almasi/Torres/bauergriffinonline.com; Venturini/bauergriffinonline.com.

CHAPTER 9
THE BEAUTY FACTOR

Page 172 Tom Munro. Model: Naty Chabanenko. **Page 175** Bill Eppridge/Time Life Pictures/Getty Images. **Page 176** Illustration by John Galliano. **Page 181** Sean Cunningham (3). **Page 184**, clockwise from top left: Jon Kopaloff/FilmMagic; Frederick M. Brown/Getty Images; Jeff Kravitz/FilmMagic; David Livingston/Getty Images. **Page 186**, clockwise from top left: Frazer Harrison/Getty Images; Larry Busacca/Getty Images; Jon Furniss/WireImage; Jason Merritt/Getty Images.

CHAPTER 10
BUILDING A FOUNDATION

Page 187 Peter Lindbergh. Model: Eniko Mihalik. **Page 189** John Springer Collection/Corbis. **Page 190:** Illustration by Jean-Paul Gaultier. **Page 195**, clockwise from top left: Darryl Patterson; Nils Friedman/Studio D; Ben Goldstein/Studio D; Darryl Patterson; Nils Friedman/Studio D. **Pages 196—197**, clockwise from top left: Nils Friedman/Studio D; Dan & Corina Lecca (3); Nils Friedman/Studio D; Julien Hekimian/WireImage; Donato Sardella/WireImage.

Cover design by Chris Thompson
Interior design by Suzanne Noli for Apartment 8H
Layout by Mia Song
Digital imaging by Erica Parente
Photo editing by Karina Dearwood
With thanks to Jennifer Dixon, Nancy Gillen, Elizabeth Hummer, Karin Kato, Aaron Leth, Lisa M. Luna, Anne Monoky, Kristina O'Neill, Alexandra Parnass, Tabatha Paterni, Gary Ponzo, Andrea Rosengarten, Sarah Strzelec, Amber Vanderzee, Anamaria Wilson

Library of Congress Cataloging-in-Publication Data
Armstrong, Lisa.
Harper's bazaar fashion : your guide to personal style / by Lisa Armstrong ;
edited by Meenal Mistry.
   p. cm.
 Includes index.
 ISBN 978-1-58816-865-8
 1. Fashion--Periodicals--History--Pictorial works. 2. Fashion--History--Pictorial works.
3. Harper's bazaar. I. Mistry, Meenal. II. Title.
 TT500.A1A75 2010
 746.9'2--dc22
                                    2010012981

10 9 8 7 6 5 4 3 2 1

Published by Hearst Books
A division of Sterling Publishing Co., Inc.
387 Park Avenue South, New York, NY 10016

Harper's Bazaar is a registered trademark of Hearst Communications, Inc.
www.harpersbazaar.com

Distributed in Canada by Sterling Publishing
c/o Canadian Manda Group, 165 Dufferin Street
Toronto, Ontario, Canada M6K 3H6

Distributed in Australia by Capricorn Link (Australia) Pty. Ltd.
P.O. Box 704, Windsor, NSW 2756 Australia

Manufactured in China
Sterling ISBN 978-1-58816-865-8

For information about custom editions, special sales, premium and corporate purchases, please contact Sterling Special Sales Department at 800-805-5489 or specialsales@sterlingpublishing.com.